Parenting Magic offers a fresh ⌐   ⌐s
you how to connect with you   ⌐ ⌐⌐ and
open more to the daily joys that are easy to overlook. It really is
magic!

Marci Shimoff – international speaker, co-founder, Your Year of
Miracles; #1 NY *Times* best-selling author of *Happy for No Reason*,
Love for No Reason and *Chicken Soup for the Woman's Soul*

What a wonderful book! It is rare and heart-warming to find a
book on parenting that is at once, wise, vulnerable, humorous,
scientific and inspiring! All this is contained within the tender
pages of *Parenting Magic*. Karen Shaw's blend of warm personal
stories as a single mom of three boys, combined with a rich
review of the most useful theories in child and adult psychology,
including the powerful Energy Alignment Method, make this
a book that will appeal to parents of all backgrounds, ages and
beliefs. Give this gift to yourself.

Bruce Cryer – founder, Renaissance Human, former CEO,
HeartMath

Conscious communication is central to my own work, which
is why I am so keen to recommend Karen's book to parents
everywhere. Our kids – the next generation – will be more
conscious, capable and grounded from being raised by more
conscious parents.

From my medical background, treating adults with addiction
and low self-worth, I understand the power of the messages we
receive from our caregivers in childhood, the knock-on effects
to their development and even the choices they make as adults. I
love that Karen has dedicated a chapter of her book to explaining
the neuroscience of child development in plain English so that
everyone can understand.

When we better understand our roles in our children's
development, we can parent more confidently and responsibly,
knowing how to pass on more of our knowledge and life lessons,
and less of our pain or anxieties.

Andrea Pennington, MD – author of *The Real Self Love Handbook*

At last a parenting book that makes sense for all parents regardless of what age their child is, or the situation they are facing. Since the beginning of time parents have been navigating unconsciously in the dark as they try to do the best by their children. With no parenthood manual, much of what we demonstrate is either moving to or away from what we have personally experienced ourselves as children.

Karen Shaw brings a new dimension to parenthood, in this messy and often times complicated modern world. Empowering parents to understand the power of their thoughts, words and actions in order to consciously navigate this parenting journey fully supported, and allowing their children the freedom to be themselves.
Kezia Luckett, Positive Psychologist, Msc – international bestselling author and motivational speaker

I absolutely loved this book, written from the heart. Karen has created the ultimate guide to bringing up happy children … a must for every parent.
Sara Lou-Ann Jones – CEO of Centre of Excellence

As parents we're gifted an important opportunity to raise the next generation of adults who have the potential to go out into the world and make it a better place. But it's not always easy, and it's often bloody hard.

Parenting Magic shows us how to practically navigate the challenges, whilst infusing the power of positive energy to lift ourselves and our children into higher levels of conscious living. A true breath of fresh air in the parenting book sector.
Kelly Pietrangeli – author of Project Me for Busy Mothers and creator of myprojectme.com

This book is a masterpiece to teach us to become wonderful parents by learning more about ourselves and our children and also how to maintain healthy happy relationships. It is written in an enjoyable way, which makes complex information easy to understand. This is the book every parent has been waiting for!
Dr. Dawn Gibbins, MBE – The Wild Grandma, www.wildgrandma.com

Karen has certainly encapsulated the art of conscious parenting between the covers of this beautiful book ... I so wish this book had been available 50+ years ago when I became a very nervous and confused parent. How differently I would have handled my challenge with Karen's gentle guidance, insight and wisdom to hand.

Jean Francis – One Spirit Interfaith Foundation

This is the book I wish I had when I became a parent. This is the book I wish I had by my side as my sons were growing up. We need to get this book into the hands of all parents ... Karen is the Marie Kondo of parenting.

Louisa Havers – transformational life and business coach, EAM mentor

Being a parent comes in all shapes and sizes, but is always the most important job in the world. The daily impact we have in our children's lives influences and shapes who they become and ultimately ripples into the generations of the future. Being a parent is a gift, but it doesn't always mean it's easy. This book is such a gift too. Every 21st century parent needs a bit of Karen's *Parenting Magic* wisdom, reassurance and new-world tools to navigate the journey of raising and nurturing another human soul.

Nicola Huelin – award-winning business coach and mentor, founder of Mpower for Mums in Business, TEDx speaker, author of *The Invisible Revolution*, *www.mpower.global*

What I love the most about this book is that it opens us all up to the possibility and the idea that there is another way. It bestows permission to embrace a different approach and shows us how. I loved every single piece of this book and can feel Karen's essence throughout it. Definitely a must-read for anyone looking for a new way who has no idea where to start.

Shari Thompson – Marketing Alchemist

A wonderful piece of work that weaves Karen's personal journey with her three boys around golden nuggets of wisdom when it comes to being a parent.

You will get 'aha' moments galore as the various scenarios we experience with our kids are explained in such an easily understandable manner ... Karen's brilliant strategic approach to parenting, in which she goes through the practical tools and techniques that empower both yourself and your kids to thrive, is just sheer 'magic'.

Mel Eves – Performance Specialist

A treasure trove of information and a new way of thinking, being and doing within parenthood. I just know that this will be a wonderful help for parents. Parenting doesn't come with a manual but this is as close as you'd get to one.

Jo Tocher – emotional loss specialist, author of *Life After Miscarriage – Your Guide to Healing After Pregnancy Loss*, EAM mentor

You will find this book to be genuinely filled with parenting magic. With pure honesty, Karen Shaw has shared personal stories to effectively convey how communication and connection create loving and supportive relationships with children. She has skilfully combined insights directly from her heart as a mother, with the vast knowledge she has gained as a professional. The beauty of her sharing results in you having the wonderful opportunity to gain the desired confidence you seek as you become a more conscious parent.

Deborah McNelis, M.Ed – Brain Insights, founder, author, international speaker and creator of Neuro-Nurturing

If you are looking for advice to parent more consciously, peacefully and with love as your compass, this book is for you. It is full of easy to use practical tips for your everyday parenting.

Gitte Winter Graugaard – author of *The Children's Meditations in my Heart*, and expert in peaceful bedtime routines

Parenting Magic

A **new** approach to behaviour & communication

Karen Shaw

Conscious Connection & Confident Parenting

First published in Great Britain by Practical Inspiration Publishing, 2020

© Karen Shaw, 2020

The moral rights of the author have been asserted.

ISBN   978-1-78860-170-2 (print)
        978-1-78860-168-9 (mobi)
        978-1-78860-169-6 (epub)

All rights reserved. This book, or any portion thereof, may not be reproduced without the express written permission of the author.

Every effort has been made to trace copyright holders and to obtain their permission for the use of copyright material. The publisher apologizes for any errors or omissions and would be grateful if notified of any corrections that should be incorporated in future reprints or editions of this book.

Practical Inspiration
PUBLISHING

MIX
Paper from
responsible sources
FSC
www.fsc.org   FSC® C013604

Dedication

To Kris, Hallam and Eden, my wonderful children, my three boys. Thank you. I love you.

Thank you to my children, my wonderful sons, for giving me the opportunity to question the status quo around the acceptance of "normal" and of what "good" parenting means. To question expectations, for our children and all humanity, and to rethink the way we measure achievement and success in life.

Contents

Foreword

At points in your life you meet someone special, unique and amazing. When you meet them you may never realize just how important they are or will become in your future. Meeting Karen was one of those for me.

My name is Yvette Taylor, first of all I am a mummy, who has been praying for this book for a long time. When out of mummy mode, people also know me as the creator of EAM – The Energy Alignment Method™. EAM is a transformational self-help tool and internationally recognized complementary therapy. Through this work I've also become an international bestselling author, speaker and coach. We lead an amazing community of people who want to make a difference in the world.

Over the last few years, we've been lucky enough to have Karen working as part of our team of Energy Alignment Method mentors, sharing her wisdom with us and more than 40,000 people as a lead coach in our programs and holding live events.

I remember meeting Karen by chance in one of my Facebook groups. Even from that moment I loved her energy, her presence and her knowledge. We spoke and instantly our connection began. I could see in her eyes and hear in her voice her passion to make a change to the lives of children and parents, sharing all she knew about parenting in a new paradigm. I never knew so much wisdom and experience could be contained in one person. We have a shared vision to impact the lives of millions of parents and children on this planet, in realizing the power we have.

Fast forward a few years, here we are and *Parenting Magic* is in your hands. Trust that you have this book for a reason. The answer you have been searching for is in here. You are in the hands of an incredible coach, teacher, guide, leader, mentor and mother. With a wealth of expertise from working for over 14 years in this space with thousands of people. She has been through the ups and downs, highs and lows of life, love and parenting. I know she has so many powerful insights to share with you.

As a parent we have THE single most important job in the world. To raise powerful, confident, happy, loving, caring, compassionate, driven children (I am sure the list goes on). It is our duty first for our children, second for society. If only we had a way to educate parents about the power they have, to shape the entire direction of their child's life. We would see such a huge shift in the whole of humanity.

It is so much easier than you may believe, too. By understanding a few powerful psychology, biology, energy and therapy principles you can make such a difference.

I know this is a key part of Karen's mission and exactly what you'll find inside this book. If only every parent was given this book, wow, what a change there would be.

Let's be real, raising a child can also be disempowering. At times it can leave you unhappy, not loving and wanting to drive away from your children, simply so you can escape! We've all been there. Yet your children feel everything that is happening in you, whether you say the words or not. It is down to us to openly, honestly communicate from a place of love.

Inside here you'll see how much of a powerful influence you can have simply by changing what you think, how you feel and what is happening in your energy.

It is invaluable as parents to understand our child's subconscious, how our words, thoughts, energy and actions are literally shaping their future.

Inside, Karen shares with you the power of your words, the impact of lies and how to manage behaviour (theirs and your own). How you can adapt your language, how to respond and not react. How to ask for what you want without the push back. And the 21 things your teenager wants to say to you (and it is not what you think!).

Put what you learn in this book into practice, then like MAGIC, you'll see your children, partner and loved ones transform in the blink of an eye. Watch them calm, open up and communicate, hear you when you ask, see how they respond to your new energy. I promise it will open your mind to the power of possibilities you have.

This is the book you have been waiting for, with a wonderful mix of science and energy. If you want a practical, grounded, honest and real-life understanding of how to positively create the best for all your family, here it is.

I'm so excited to see this book as I know how long it has been a part of her vision, we've ALL been praying for it for some time. The first of many books that I hope Karen will write, as she boldly steps into her mission of changing the way we parent.

Working alongside Karen as part of the EAM community is a blessing in itself. I know you'll feel the magic of her work in the words in this book too. This is so much more than positive or conscious parenting, this is transformational family magic.

Every parent needs this book. It is the one you have been waiting for.

To your continued success.

Yvette Taylor,
BSC H IIHHT,
creator of the Energy Alignment Method,
author of *The Ultimate Self-Help Book*

Acknowledgements

I want to express my gratitude to those who have touched my life. I would not have written this book if I hadn't learnt and experienced everything I have in my life so far.

I want to thank my children. Kris, Hal and Eden who have given me the reason to write this book. Have given me purpose, provided challenges, dilemmas and distractions and also a great sense of joy, love and pride.

My parents Edward and Elizabeth Shaw for being the best parents they could be, providing a safe and secure home and childhood for myself and my siblings. To those siblings, Lesley, Tony and Paul, whose diverse personalities, opinions and contributions to my life are appreciated and matter and who are very important to me.

To two wonderful teachers, who introduced me to the power of words, to poetry, English literature and language, to drama and a love of theatre. Mr. Kelly, John Kelly, my junior four teacher whose enthusiasm for choral speaking and poetry rubbed off and inspired me. Who sadly is no longer with us. To a truly lovely lady Mrs Baxter (Pat Baxter at the time, now Pat Fuller) my 'elocution' teacher. Who introduced me to Shakespeare and how emotive the written and spoken word can be. For her encouragement and belief in me.

To Yvette Taylor, who has inspired and supported me, nudged, cajoled and encouraged me. To my EAM family for their support, especially Jo Tocher who shared many a long car journey listening to my stories and ideas, that have now made their way into this book.

Special thanks and eternal gratitude to Brenda Howard, a more than dear and valued friend, for being there through many highs and lows in my life. For supporting me every step of the way, even when she thought I was mad!

To Alison Jones and her team at Practical Inspiration alongside the team at Newgen. For guidance, patience and support.

To all family and friends, not mentioned by name, know you are all important to me and have contributed to who I am and therefore integral to the creation and completion of this book.

Introduction

Your children are not your children
They are the sons and daughters of Life's longing for itself.
They come through you but not from you,
And though they are with you yet they belong not to you.
You may give them your love but not your thoughts,
For they have their own thoughts.
You may house their bodies but not their souls,
For their souls dwell in the house of tomorrow,
Which you cannot visit, not even in your dreams.

Kahlil Gibran, The Prophet[1]

My children's challenges and difficulties within the mainstream education system and realm of health and learning highlighted a need, a necessity to think outside the box, find another way and look at things differently. Out of my challenges with them as a mum and single parent arose the curiosity to look for solutions and answers to questions that I know many ask. "Is there another way, a better way?" "What else can I do?" "Am I doing the right thing?!"

In this book, I offer my opinion and share what has worked for me, with the hope it will make sense and give some comfort and solutions. I know every experience I have had, and every person who has been part of those experiences, has taught me something and helped shape who I am now, how I think and the way I look at the world. A world of unlimited potential ready to be unleashed when we break down barriers that are only confines and constricts of

---

[1] Kahlil Gibran *The Prophet* (Suezteo Enterprises 2019).

the mind, outdated ways of thinking and being that are holding us and our children prisoners. It is definitely time to set ourselves and the children free. "Setting the children free" was an alternative subtitle for this book: I want our children to be free from the constraints of outdated methods of parenting, from the pressure that we put on ourselves and them to conform to a belief system and way of parenting that can cause more damage than we realize. It was also the reply my youngest son, Eden, gave to the headmistress at his special needs school after being asked what he thought he was doing when he had enlisted the help of his classmates to remove the school gate!

My wish is to enable a generation of parents to really be able to connect and communicate with their children in a conscious and confident way. To provide a new approach to behaviour and communication that can then be passed on, so their children can do the same and that this continues through the generations. To introduce a new paradigm in parenting, to instigate a fundamental change in the approach to parenting and alter the underlying and prevalent assumptions of what parenting is.

I aim to guide you through this book so you can Be, Do and Say things in a way that will allow, enable and empower you to have the best relationship with your children, to be the best you. To help them reach their full potential, have a happy childhood and for you to enjoy parenting and have a happy family life.

I have provided a *Parenting Magic* journal template at the back of the book for you to use and an explanation of how to use it. Pick one new tip or technique you've learnt that you will start to implement.

There is also an A–Z of *Parenting Magic*. Bite size and easily digestible chunks of advice or insight for each letter of the alphabet, for a quick read if you're pushed for time.

I have a vision of a world where all children are able to shine their unique brilliance in the world. Where we are raising happy, fulfilled adults. Let's be part of a movement that's dedicated to making that happen.

Part 1

From unconscious to conscious parenting

I used to think that the difference between being conscious and unconscious was that if you were awake you were conscious and if you were asleep (or knocked out!) you were unconscious. An accurate interpretation, though some time ago I learnt that so many of us are walking round awake, or at least not asleep in the conventional way and yet still not very "consciously" aware at all. This is the way a lot of people are living their lives and certainly parenting, with a lack of awareness of what they are doing and the effect it has on their children. A society living under a mass hypnosis, believing that what we see is the way it is and has to be, that this is reality, happy to keep the status quo, or if not so happy, not sure what to do about it. A lot of people are not consciously aware of what we human beings truly are or what we are capable of. The untapped potential and abilities we possess. Not aware either of the impact on our children of how we Be, Do, or Say things, and are unconsciously conscious. This could get complicated, so bear with me!

I started to be aware of how much of what I was doing was unconscious when I took my Neuro Linguistic Programming (NLP) training in 2006 and was introduced to the "Ladder of Consciousness" accredited to Noel Burch, creating and identifying the four stages of learning. These are:

- Unconsciously incompetent. We don't know what we don't know.
- Consciously incompetent. We do know what we don't know.
- Consciously competent. We do know what we know and can "consciously" carry it out (i.e. with some effort).
- Unconsciously competent. What we know is so ingrained, we do it without thinking.

Think about the process of learning to drive, for instance. When we have been driving for a while we get to the stage of unconscious competence and don't have to think about it, we can do it on auto pilot. So much of what we do is unconscious, we do it automatically, without thinking about it. It's become habit. Sometimes good and sometimes not so good!

We can be alert and aware of our surroundings though not really aware of, or have knowledge of, the deeper implications of how our thoughts, words, actions and behaviours really influence and affect us and our children, so effectively unconscious and back to not knowing what we don't know. It's time to be aware.

Chapter 1

Becoming a parent

It takes time to become a conscious parent and it is a process. It involves looking at and changing the way we think about parenting, our children and ourselves. The old paradigm of parenting is outdated, where we think we are totally responsible for our children's lives and choices. Where adults think they know best and must be obeyed (okay, not all parents think like this), fitting their children into an education system that doesn't suit them and isn't really working. Where the emphasis is still on academia and not on teaching life skills. We're not preparing our children well enough to deal with emotional and mental health. We don't teach enough about positive effective communication, relationships or finances. Skills that are so necessary to get on in life. We have a limited understanding of what the parent–child relationship is, what it can be and how to get the best out of it for all concerned. We have a lot of unhappy children, who are not able to fulfil their potential. They have pressure from society, peers, parents and school and we have a lot of unhappy, stressed out parents struggling with parenting. We have more children presenting with mental and emotional health issues than ever before. According to the NSPCC, in 2018 the most common reason for calls and sessions given was for mental health and emotional issues.[1]

---

[1] www.nspcc.org.uk/keeping-children-safe/our-services/childline/ [accessed April 2020].

There certainly isn't a magic wand, although I can promise that if you apply all the tools, tips and techniques in this book and take on board another way of looking at your children and yourselves, you will see results. Happy, well rounded, respectful, loving children who are comfortable in their own skin, in the world. Confident, self-assured and knowing who they are. You will have a more peaceful time parenting. This book is for those who wish to be conscious, soulful and aligned parents. Everything I share with you is what I have learnt and put into practice, and has led to me having a fantastic relationship with my boys. Each child is unique and has a zone of genius, a brilliance that is waiting to emerge. It can with the right support. *Parenting Magic* will help you be the best parent, the best you, you can be. It will help you enjoy your parenting journey and lead a happy family life. I want you to love your time with your children and value them for their uniqueness. I ask you to have an open mind, persevere and have patience. It will be worth it.

An unconditional offer

I want to take you back to a Thursday evening, 5th April 2012. I lay in bed, alone and unable to sleep. I had been, by this time, divorced for almost eleven years and still single. I lay thinking about what had happened that morning. My youngest son, Eden, had received a letter from Trinity Saint David's University of Wales, Lampeter, offering him an unconditional place there in September 2012 to study History and Archaeology. It was a great day, it was a fantastic day, we were so pleased, so happy. We were thrilled, as you can imagine, and when I explain Eden's journey up to this point you'll understand why.

Looking back, I counted and realized that I had gone through 53 previous April 5ths and over 2,500 Thursdays and I don't remember any as clearly as this one!

I lay there in bed that night reflecting on Eden's good news. I thought about his achievement, what an accomplishment it was, bearing in mind his early educational life. The early years of his life altogether were fraught with challenges.

I was compelled to get out of bed and go and get Eden's blue box file, where I had lovingly collected the history of his journey, including his home made comic books, Mother's Day cards, paintings and drawings, medical and educational reports, letters etc., and as I revisited some of those incredibly difficult times it really hit me what an extraordinary journey he'd had (we'd had). What a remarkable young man he was and what a story was there to tell.

In the blue box file I found a Home/School book, this was a vital link between home and school, written in daily by a member of staff at the language unit and additional needs school Eden attended and either myself or Adrian, Eden's dad.

I opened one of these little exercise books and on the first page read the following: "After consideration, Miss Johnson [Head teacher] has decided the school has a certain responsibility for the incident and realize that Eden must have seen the workmen who were at school a few days ago take the school gate off to get to the manhole under it to do some work…"

It all came flooding back to me, I remembered Eden had enlisted the help of some of the other children to lift the gate off its hinges, so they could "escape"! When he was asked what he was doing he said "Setting the children free". He was eight at the time. He was good at problem solving. I think he knew unconsciously that school wasn't always the best place for children and he saw an opportunity to do something about it. It's this incident that inspired the working title of this book. "Setting the Children Free" is what I want to do.

I read of many other occasions that made me laugh and cry. His magic trick of making a five pound note disappear. This came to light when I got the following note from school one Monday. "We are returning a five pound note that Eden had in school on Friday, it should have come home then, sorry we forgot to put it in his bag. He said it was part of a magic trick!"

My reply, the next day, was "Thank you for returning it, Adrian and I knew there was a five pound note on the kitchen side and wondered what had happened to it. We asked Eden about it and what he meant, it was part of a magic trick? His reply, 'Well I made it disappear, didn't I?' ... True! We also talked to him about taking things that didn't belong to him!"

There were also reminders of the kind things he did. School let us know he had won a selection box in a raffle one Christmas and immediately shared it with his classmates, making sure there was one bar he could bring home for his brother, Hallam. His letter to Father Christmas in 2002 after I was divorced: "Dear Father Christmas, if I am good please may I have something for my mum. Thank you. Love Eden." How touching is that?

There were notes of Eden having a very bad day and being angry and disruptive, not able to learn his alphabet or spell even two or three letter words. Scribbling furiously on paper, screwing it up and throwing it, throwing toys and knocking chairs over. Hating himself so much he would gouge at his cheeks with his fingers, cry and say he wanted to be dead. Reading all this brought it back and was heart-breaking to revisit, so where he had got to, being offered a place at university, was really wonderful and a lot of what I had learnt through NLP, hypnotherapy, energy therapies and my own personal and spiritual development had helped. What I put into practice is what I'm going to share in this book.

A different experience

Eden is my third and youngest child (all boys) and did not conform or follow the expected pattern of development or behaviour. He was brilliantly unique, as all children are, they're just not allowed to express it most of the time. He found it difficult to do as he was told, sit still, complete tasks without being distracted and was intrigued and interested in things other than were on the agenda! When Eden first went to primary school, the Headmaster there was not flexible or accommodating and definitely not very understanding or tolerant. When Eden was in reception class I remember having a conversation with the Headmaster about Eden's behaviour and how the Headmaster said he would not have a four year old do as Eden did in his school and he had to conform and learn to behave. He did behave… just not as the Head wanted!

For example, before Christmas one year Eden's father and I were called into the Head's office for him to tell us he thought it would be better if Eden didn't appear in the nativity play as he wouldn't behave. We didn't agree and said we wanted Eden to be in the play. He had been cast as one of the Three Kings and was very happy with his cloak and crown that they had made in school, all the boys had the same kind of crown. Then Eden's dad brought a flashing crown back from a trip to Blackpool and naturally Eden wanted to wear this, which he wasn't allowed to do.

We got round it by getting Eden to wear the home made crown on his head and the flashing lights crown as a belt, it clipped together at the back. He was happy enough doing this. When the play was in full swing and it got to the part where Mary and Joseph are told "There's no room at the Inn", Eden suddenly perked up, looked very puzzled and leapt into action, going to get Mary and Joseph, leading them to where he was on the stage saying "There is room, there's room here and here!" This is exactly what makes school nativity plays so special, and we were so pleased and happy Eden had been included. Eden wasn't purposely naughty, he just had a different perspective on the world; what he did made perfect sense to him.

Looking at things with a different perspective, or from slightly outside the box, to the way the majority would think was something Eden was good at. When he was about four or five years old, he and I were walking to school one morning. He was wearing a royal blue sweatshirt, his school uniform, and I had on a Kingfisher-turquoise coloured sweatshirt, a Rosemary Conley one to be exact, since I was on my way to teach a class after taking Eden to school. I was a Rosemary Conley Diet and Fitness Instructor at that time. He looked at our tops and said "Your top is the same colour as mine with a bit of the sun broken off and rolled up in it." That was one way of explaining it.

Eden's way of being was eventually diagnosed as Asperger's syndrome. He was on the autistic spectrum and had other disorders associated with it, including ADHD, dyslexia, semantic and pragmatic language disorder and social and behavioural difficulties. He was given an educational statement of special needs and found a place at a special needs school.

Eden did well at his special language unit school and loved his teachers, especially his Miss Seagrave (he always referred to her as "my Miss Seagrave") and Mrs Morris, who helped him enormously. It was when he was about ten years old and having to think of which secondary school he wanted to go to that he decided he wanted to go to an "ordinary" secondary school. I embarked on a journey to get him into mainstream school. It wasn't easy. I had to persuade and convince people that Eden could cope. He did get a place at a local mainstream school and a lot of support was put into place for him. It was difficult for him. At eleven years old when he started Siddal Moor Sports College (not that Eden had any particular interest in sport, it was the local school and had a good reputation) he could barely read or write three-letter words. I often would look out of the window in the afternoon to see Eden returning from school, looking like he was under a cloud, not happy at all. I would hear the front door open, his school bag get thrown or kicked down the hall, he would then come into the kitchen, throw himself down on a chair at the kitchen table and start what had become a usual rant about himself and school. "I hate that school, I can't do anything, I'm so stupid, I can't learn..." and more self-destructive comments. It was a tough time for him and I am so grateful that I was able to put into place a lot I had learnt from NLP, hypnotherapy and personal development to help Eden and myself. I changed the way I thought, behaved and parented. I have shared here some of the tools and techniques I used that have made such a difference to my life, to my relationship with my boys. People often comment on how lovely our relationship is and may even say "You're so lucky." I am grateful and feel blessed, and though I didn't have a magic wand and it didn't happen overnight, what I did put into practice has worked... like magic!

Conditions

Eden's unconditional offer from university made me think about the phrase and realize, that's what we make our children when we invite them into our lives, when we have them, an unconditional offer, and yet very soon we start to put conditions on that offer. Think about it, how perfect is our newborn baby? We do love them unconditionally. We don't expect anything from them, it's enough for them to just be, we are grateful they have made it and we are full of that love and adoration for them. Think about that newborn baby, a baby a few weeks old or even a few months old, lying in their cot all snuggly and cosy, beautiful skin, rosy cheeks. We don't criticize them for not doing very much round the house, or for not having much hair yet, we don't think "Oh they need to lose a few inches around the middle." We find it easy to accept them just as they are. We're not *expecting* of them as much as *accepting* of them. That changes and as children get older we do expect, naturally, it's part of growing up and we find it more difficult to accept as easily. A baby can do little wrong. Everything they do is cute, funny, adorable and they are forgiven all sorts of behaviour that as they get older they are told is wrong or not accepted. Praise is heaped on the baby who brings up wind. Then a little later, burping is rude, not acceptable. When a toddler is heard using swear words or inappropriate phrases, this is often met with amusement and laughter (out of shock sometimes, I know) then they are told they mustn't say that. Confusing, isn't it? Who's changed? Think about it. They haven't. They are behaving the same as they always have or copying behaviour they have seen or repeating what they have heard. We change our behaviour and start to point out more and more of what they are doing wrong and often we praise them less and less for what they are doing right. Is it the malaise of society, to look at what's wrong more than what's right? We do this so often, look at the negative and not the positive. How often have you heard people say, when asked how they are, "Not bad"? If someone says that to me I often say "I asked how you are, not how you're not" or "If you're not bad, what are you?"

We put so much pressure on children (and ourselves) to behave in a certain way instead of accepting more of who and what they are. I don't mean accept unwanted behaviour. We have to have boundaries and agreements in place and also make sure they know that behaviour is separate from who they are. Behaviour is what they do, not who they are. So whatever they do, we will always love them, though not necessarily approve, like or be happy with what they have done. As they grow up they learn that they are expected to do certain things, behave in certain ways, do well at school, do their best and that's all fine, they will usually naturally want to. We don't want them to grow up thinking that they are only loved if they achieve certain standards, grades, get into a certain school or do what we want them to. If we are constantly setting milestones, goals or targets for them to reach, this can instil an unconscious belief that they are not already enough in themselves, that they have to achieve something outside of themselves instead of us helping them realize they are already and always enough. That they are perfect the way they are right now and help and encourage them to find a way for who they truly are to emerge. The oak is already in the tree.[2]

If we push, coerce or strongly encourage our children to follow a certain path because we think it's the right thing to do, we can actually be hindering them finding their own

---

[2] You can read more about this acorn theory in James Hillman *The Soul's Code: In Search of Character and Calling* (Bantam 1997) and Derek Rydall *Emergence: Seven Steps for Radical Life Change* (Beyond Words Publishing 2015).

purpose and passion and inadvertently be minimizing their success and fulfilment. My belief is you are here to assist the unveiling of who and what your child is meant to be, what their true nature is, not what you want because you think it's best, not what you want them to be because it's what you wanted and never got the chance.

More accepting, less expecting.

Love is the answer

Your child's first experience of anything is from you. Love, authority, kindness, or lack of. You are the first example of the fundamental emotions we experience (or their first primary caregiver is) and impact on them so much, with what you show them, teach them and as we'll explore, with the energy you emit. In short, who you Be, what you Do and what you Say all have an energy, a vibrational frequency, and this sets their vibration level. There's a lot to this parenting business, far more than just what we do. Not an easy job. Michael Beckwith (Dr Michael Bernard Beckwith) founder of Agape International Spiritual Center, talks about raising children as being like trying to change a tyre while the car is still moving, and I love Wayne Dyer's quote: "I used to have at least eight theories about raising children when I had none and now I have eight children, I have no theories!"

When we show our displeasure or are angry or annoyed with our children they can feel that we are withholding love, which we are. It may feel justified. Let them know we don't like, approve of or condone something, definitely, as long as we have a strong foundation in place and they know they are still and always loved. It's easy to say "of course they know they're loved", perhaps they still need to be told and shown this on a regular basis.

Love is an emotion (an energy in motion) and is one of the higher vibrational frequencies that can be felt. When we are not vibrating that frequency because of something our child has done, or something that has happened, and we are experiencing another emotion, e.g. anger, disappointment, frustration, etc., these are emotions of a lower frequency and are felt by our children.

Children need to know how much you love them and how much they mean to you throughout their lives, through the tots, teens and in-betweens and it can get more challenging, especially when they are teenagers, when you may feel, as I did, you are living with someone from a different planet!

When we withdraw love, or it appears we have to them, it leads to them becoming confused about their relationship with us. "Am I not loved now?" This is where fear sets in, a child becomes fearful of not being loved. Fear is also experienced by the parent when there are too many expectations of their child, to do certain things at a certain age. They become anxious if their child isn't walking as early as other babies or toddlers. Isn't potty trained or talking yet. Worried and fearful they aren't able to say their alphabet yet, read, ride a bike, swim, etc. They worry for their child, what if they do this or don't do that and compare them to other children. There is also a fear of being judged by others that they have somehow failed as a parent (this may not be a conscious thought, though is often running at an unconscious level).

We see this playing out, I believe, in "helicopter parenting", where parents constantly keep a close eye on what their child does. In 1990, child development researchers Foster Cline and Jim Fay coined the term to refer to a parent who hovers over a child, like a helicopter, and behaves in a way that isn't conducive to raising an independent child.

The metaphor appeared earlier in 1969 in the bestselling book *Between Parent & Teenager* by Dr Haim Ginott, which mentions a teen who complains that "Mother hovers over me like a helicopter".

There is also a term "lawnmower parenting", those who are one step ahead of their kids and actually already laying the path, smoothing the way, sorting out what their kids will be doing. There are those who exercise a little too much control and are moulding their children, often into doing what they, the parent, thinks the child should do or wants the child to do and maybe even pushing a bit, and that's exhibiting something known as "snowplough parenting"!

We often don't know how best to support our children, to help them feel secure and confident in life, to make good choices for themselves and recognize and follow the things that will help them grow up to be happy and healthy and reach their full potential. There are still parents who believe that they do know what's best for their child, as they have lived longer and have more experience of life. Their child's life is not theirs, they are on a different path and our job is to help them find and explore theirs. It may be very different from ours. It's easy to become a parent, not always easy to parent well. We don't have to pass an exam to become one, take any training and we don't get a manual that tells us what to do!

An unconditional offer like Eden's place at university means no strings attached. Often parents tell me they love their children unconditionally and they would do anything for them. This very often isn't true. We so often say things that are not true, not really when we analyse them, though I know parents believe this when they say it. I want us to start realizing how often we lie to ourselves and how what we say is taken on by our unconscious mind (and our child's) and has far-reaching and long-lasting effects.

> *It's easy to become a parent, not always easy to parent well.*

A parent often says "I would do anything for my child." That probably isn't true. We all have values and boundaries and there will be things you wouldn't do even for your child. I'm not saying you don't believe it when you say it, just that when you do think about it you'll know there are certain things you just would not do! The unconscious mind is always listening and it knows this isn't true. A lot of what we say isn't, language is often inadequate or incorrect. We do lie to ourselves and to our children and the unconscious mind holds on to it! (For more on this, see Part 4 Chapter 6, section entitled Tell the truth.)

Why become a parent?

Too often we have no plan before we set out for how we are going to parent. Did you have the discussion with your partner about it? Or if a single parent did you know clearly how you were going to do it? I certainly didn't. With no manual or instruction book and not really having thought far enough ahead as to what we will put in place, it's no wonder it can be tricky. This may sound like an odd question, though interesting to see what answers you'll give, "Why did you have children?" A lot of clients I've worked with don't really know. "I always just wanted children", or "I thought my biological clock was running out, so thought I'd better hurry up", or "I wanted a baby" are replies I hear a lot.

Why else become a parent? So we can give love to a creation that has come from the love and intimacy we have for another human being? Is it to help populate this planet (or over populate it!), to perpetuate the loving relationship we have with our partner, our parents, or to have a relationship with our child we didn't have with our parents? To continue a family name? We want to create new life and share in the joy, pride, love and all that a baby can bring. The point of it (and points can be sharp and hurt, as being a parent can) is for us to learn and grow and is, I believe, amongst all the other reasons, perhaps the main one. Our children are here to teach us, as much as, if not more than, we are here to teach them! They are here to push our buttons so we can question what it is that we are believing, thinking, that has set us off, triggered us, and it gives us the opportunity to change things. Something has offended the ego when we find ourselves saying "It shouldn't be like this", "They can't speak to me like that" or "They are not getting away with that". These kinds of responses come from us believing things that do not really serve us or our children, it's our outdated programming. Think about what happens when you get mad at them, or are upset by what they've done or not done. It isn't them, it's behaviour, so ask why has this made me so mad, angry, upset, e.g. if you get really annoyed that they aren't listening to you, where else in your life are you not being listened to, heard? Were you listened to as a child? It's their behaviour that has triggered your reaction, because you have negative energy and emotions in you about not being heard, it's happened before, it's happening in another area of your life and this has risen to the surface and been released. If they ignore you, take no notice of your advice, opinion, don't do as you ask and you react to this, you have experienced this before somewhere or are experiencing it elsewhere, your opinion not valued, you're not listened to or heard. As parents it's for us to be aware of the reasons we become triggered. It's our opportunity to grow. As our children grow up, they are also growing us up at the same time.

> "If there is anything that we wish to change in the child, we should first examine it and see whether it is not something that could better be changed in ourselves."
>
> Carl Jung

The point of parenting (a spiritual perspective)

You may have made a conscious decision to have a child, or you may not have and it just happened. Whichever way, your child is here and I believe you did choose, as did your child, at a higher level, a different level of consciousness, for this to be so now, for them to make their appearance in this physical world at this time. An agreement was made in the wonderful world of the unconscious, at the collective consciousness level which is so much more than only human form, prior to physical existence and inhabiting a body. The soul, spirit, energy phase made a contract for it to be so. Whether you believe in previous lives or not doesn't matter. The practical tools and tips here will work. At a scientific level the whole energy thing makes sense. A scientist will say about energy, "It can't be created, or destroyed, it just is. It's in form, through form and always will be." So even if something is destroyed or deteriorates, it doesn't disappear, the energy of it remains, it transmutes and transforms, it still exists. Interestingly if you ask a theologian or religious person about God you get very much the

As our children grow up, they are also growing us up at the same time.

same reply. I think they are talking about the same thing with a different label. So when a body is no longer here in living form, there is an energy that still is, somewhere, circulating back into the ether to become something else, utilized again.[3]

---

[3] For more on this subject, see Robert Schwartz *Courageous Souls: Do We Plan Our Life Challenges Before Birth?* (Whispering Winds Press 2006) and Derek and Tara Sutphen *Soul Agreements: Explain Your Life and Loves* (Hampton Roads Publishing Co. 2005).

Chapter 2

How to become a conscious parent

Oxygen mask thinking

On a plane you will always hear the cabin crew, when giving their safety demonstration, tell adults to put the oxygen mask on themselves first before putting it on anyone else, even children. You have to be able to take care of them, you are no good to them if you're unconscious (I mean that in every sense of the word!).

It's the same with parenting, be well and truly conscious, take care of you first and be the best you are able to be, then you will be the best parent you can be. You owe it to yourself and your children to look after yourself in the best way you can. It isn't selfish to put yourself first. It is important to have quality time for you, and you and your partner if you have one. Create balance and harmony in your life to have the time for all you want to do and not spend too much time in any one area to the detriment of another. When we take care of ourselves, look after our health, get enough sleep, eat well and exercise, we are setting that example to our children. We show them that we value ourselves and encourage them to do the same.

We often hear people say they haven't got their home—work balance right. Often, the parents I work with say they feel guilty because they know their life is out of balance, too much time at work, or doing work-related things, and not being able to give quality time to their children. Though balance is what's often aimed for, picture a pair of old fashioned scales like the Scales of Justice, when they are balanced, whatever is on each scale is equally weighted. While this is what people often say they want, balance means no movement, it's static, and we don't want to become static and staid, we benefit from variety. We want movement, flow and harmony in our life.

Do things for you and learn to say "No", not just to your children to other people, too. Sometimes it can be difficult. Learn to say no without feeling guilty and making excuses. It's important to not feel under pressure and stress. We release cortisol when we're under too much stress and get angry. Cortisol is a hormone associated with stress, it's a necessary hormone to get us moving, out of bed, out of danger, though now we don't need to release as much because we're not running away from sabretooth tigers. Too much cortisol isn't helpful or healthy. Chances are on a bad day, there will be several occasions that cause you to release cortisol. Because you will have released a second or third lot before the first lot has had a chance to dissipate you are constantly topping it up and it isn't doing you any good. It's important to look after yourself and do what's right for you too, not just for others.

A basket of apples

There's a lovely children's book *Have You Filled a Bucket today*, by Carol McCloud. It talks about everyone having a happiness bucket and how we can fill our own and other people's by doing kind things. It's a guide to daily happiness. I advocate what it says, we can always do kind, loving things to help ourselves and others feel good. I also know we want our children to grow up not just doing things to please others and we have a right to say no and know when we have done enough. I encourage children and parents to have a basket (or bucket if you like) full of apples or goodies and imagine giving them away every time we do something for others or say yes to something and have a finite number so that there is a point where you can say, as I often did to my kids or other people, "Sorry, I've no more apples left today."

In this very fast-paced society, it's more important than ever to look after ourselves, take time to be calm and slow down. Meditation is so beneficial and there are lots of ways to meditate. Guided meditations, CDs to buy, downloads available and a host of apps. David Lynch, director of *Twin Peaks* and films such as *Eraserhead, Mullholland Drive, Blue Velvet* and lots more (those of a certain age will remember) runs The David Lynch Foundation, advocating the benefits of meditation and how it can help heal traumatic stress disorders. We need to be in the best state possible to be the best parent.

Aim to have your life as uncomplicated and uncluttered as possible. De-clutter, everywhere. Home and mind. Have a clean, calm environment. If it seems overwhelming, make a plan and do a bit at a time.

Get rid of any unnecessary items, sort cupboards, drawers, attic, garage. It all makes sense, you feel so much better and in control. These activities will release feel good chemicals: dopamine, serotonin, oxytocin and endorphins (see Part 4 Chapter 5, section entitled Understanding our happy chemicals). And as everything is energy (we'll explore that shortly) think about all the energy tied up in things, possessions, etc., and not always good energy. Feng shui is based on the flow of energy and how important that is in a home. Take care of your environment, you and, of course, your children and let them know you care.

Let them know you care

They don't care how much you know until they know how much you care. Teddy Roosevelt is attributed with saying "Nobody cares how much you know until they know how much you care", and James Maxwell, author of several leadership books, believed this too. It's the same in parenting. Let them know you care.

The care that comes from really being interested in them, what they like, and are interested in. Caring for them isn't just about housing them, feeding them, clothing them, caring for them physically, it is much more than that. Abraham Harold Maslow (1908–1970) was an American psychologist best known for creating Maslow's hierarchy of needs, a theory of psychological health predicated on fulfilling innate human needs in priority, culminating in self-actualization.[1] He stated that the basic needs of any human being are the physiological needs, and until these are met they can't function or achieve at any other level. He explains the following:

1. **Physiological needs** – these are biological requirements for human survival, e.g. air, food, drink, shelter, clothing, warmth, procreation, sleep. If these needs are not satisfied the human body cannot function optimally. Maslow considered physiological needs the most important because

---

[1] Saul McLeod Maslow's hierarchy of needs, available from www.simplypsychology.org/maslow.html [accessed April 2020].

all the other needs become secondary until these needs are met.

2. **Safety needs** – protection from elements, security, order, law, stability, freedom from fear.

3. **Love and belongingness needs** – after physiological and safety needs have been fulfilled, the third level of human needs is social and involves feelings of belongingness. The need for interpersonal relationships motivates behaviour. Examples include friendship, intimacy, trust, and acceptance, receiving and giving affection and love. Affiliating, being part of a group (family, friends, work).

4. **Esteem needs** – which Maslow classified into two categories: (i) esteem for oneself (dignity, achievement, mastery, independence) and (ii) the desire for reputation or respect from others (status, prestige). Maslow indicated that the need for respect or reputation is most important for children and adolescents and precedes real self-esteem or dignity.

5. **Self-actualization needs** – realizing personal potential, self-fulfilment, seeking personal growth and peak experiences. A desire "to become everything one is capable of becoming".

Give them your full attention

Remember to be present. Not simply saying "Hmmm" when they are speaking to us, while we're busy texting on the phone. They want and need our full attention, eye contact and interest in them. This is intensive care. It's easy for them to build up a limiting belief that they're not important when they experience that lack of interest. If it really isn't the time for much conversation, let them know that. It only takes a couple of seconds to stop what you're doing, look at them and tell them "I'm very busy at the moment and as soon as I've done this I'll be able to talk to you", or whatever it is they want you to do. I don't believe we should put them first all the time, or neglect what we want to do in favour of what they want. It's about finding a balance. This lets them know where they stand. They get used to you having rights and needs and a healthy relationship is formed.

The best present you can give your child is be it!

Carl Rogers' (American psychologist, 1902–1987) reflective listening is a good habit to get into.[2] You paraphrase back what has just been said to you so that you make sure you have it right. You can ask your child to repeat back to you what you have just said, to check that they heard and ask if they understand. Do this with eye contact and not while doing something else.

Another thing he taught and talked about was unconditional positive regard.

Unconditional positive regard

Where parents and significant others accept and love the person for what they are. Positive regard is not withdrawn if the person does something considered wrong or makes a mistake. The consequences of unconditional positive regard are that the person feels free to try things out and make mistakes. People who are able to self-actualize are more likely to have received unconditional positive regard from others, especially their parents, care givers and teachers in childhood.

---

[2] Carl Rogers *Client Centred Therapy* (Constable & Robinson 2003).

Conditional positive regard

This is where positive regard, such as praise and approval, depend upon the child, e.g. behaving in ways that the parents think correct. Hence the child is not loved for the person they are, but on condition that they behave only in ways approved by the parent(s). At the extreme, a person who constantly seeks approval from other people is likely only to have experienced conditional positive regard as a child.

To care fully for our children means caring about what they're thinking, feeling and doing, caring about their emotions. Care about what they are interested in; you don't have to be interested in it, just in them being interested in whatever it is.

We can show we care in the way we are with our children. How we Be with them as well as by what we Do and Say. My three main focus areas of Parenting Magic are offering ways to Be, Do and Say things differently to achieve the results you want.

Benefits of letting them know you care

It will:

- Raise their self-esteem, self-worth and self-confidence.
- Help you reap what you sow. When you show them how much you care, they'll show you how much they care about you. Remember, children will do as you do not as you say (though more of that when you put the tools and tips in this book into place!). They will become what you and their environment show them and allow them to be, so set a good example.

- Build a stronger connection between you and your child.
- Help you to be able to separate the person from the behaviour your child is displaying, by remembering you still love the child, it's the behaviour you don't love!
- Encourage communication and openness.
- Allow them to build up their trust so they can allow you into their world, at any age.

Seven steps to let them know you care

1. Tell them and keep telling them you love them and just as importantly, show them: actions speak louder than words.
2. Praise them for what they do well, even if it isn't as you would have done it, and avoid telling them how you would have done it! (Learn to deliver a feedback sandwich, see Part 3 Chapter 4, Magic language). Let's lose criticism, think of it more as instruction or guidance.
3. Compliment them and mean it, e.g. when they've made an effort to look good even when you think that shirt doesn't really go with those trousers, or you don't like the colour of that lipstick.
4. Show interest in what they are interested in. No dissing what they like. Say, "I'm glad to see you reading" (whatever it is, well, within reason) or "It's great you're taking an interest in music", even if it's not your cup of tea.
5. Be clear they understand it's their behaviour you don't like and not them. Say "I don't like what you've done" or "That behaviour is selfish".
6. Be present and give them the time they need to know you care, e.g. when they want to show you

something or tell you something, or just want to share something, to spend time with you. Be aware of telling them "Not now, I'm busy": you may genuinely be busy, though what your child hears is "I'm not important" or "What I have to say isn't important". What we say to our children has a huge impact on them. Alter what you say slightly: "I'm a bit busy right now and as soon as I've finished I'll come and talk to you", reassure them of your interest and that they do matter.

7. Say yes more often and mean it. Very often a child will ask if they can do something, paint, go outside, play with a certain friend and without thinking we say no. What we often mean is not now, or I don't want you to, because the truth is they actually can do or are able to do that thing! This confuses the unconscious mind that knows they *can*; they know they are able to do it and so the lies begin. Say yes first and then qualify it, with something like "when we've finished tidying up" or "yes, tomorrow" or "another time". Let them hear the word yes more often.

One way I put showing how much I cared into practice was by consistently putting notes in my son's packed lunches. When a Bakewell tart was part of the lunch I cut out a circular piece of white paper to fit exactly over the icing part of the cake with a hole for the cherry and wrote in a spiral round it! It doesn't matter too much what you say as long as it's positive. I did the same when he had Neapolitan Bakewell tarts with pink icing (I used a pink post it note, cut a shape out of it in the middle to go over the little bit of chocolate flake on top). And this was when he was 17!

When I was helping Eden with his reading (Pokémon and PlayStation magazines!) it showed my interest, my care, and helped him improve his reading. If your child plays a lot of video games show interest and wear rose coloured specs, see the positives in it. It improves dexterity, fine motor control, encourages a desire to do well, to achieve and be successful and self-motivated. Each level of achievement triggers the dopamine effect, which stimulates the happy neurochemicals that motivate the need and desire to play more and achieve more. These small goals in this game-playing wire the brain and this can lead to bigger picture goals and achievements being reached. I'm not advocating excessive game-playing or that this should take over their lives. Boundaries are still needed with this activity and close monitoring of games being played is strongly advisable. Also limited screen time is healthy too. There's evidence to say that too much screen time is not good for children (well anyone, actually). I am encouraging you to be interested in whatever it is your child is interested in and find some good in it. Be curious about why they're interested, what it is they like, enjoy or get from it.

Praise and compliments

It's important to encourage our children and let them know that they are doing well, achieving and accomplishing things. Empty praise isn't very helpful. Make it meaningful. Not just "Oh that's good" when they show you a picture they have drawn, find something you think is good or that you like, such as "I really like the colours you've chosen" or "I really love the way you've drawn the branches on the trees", and mean it.

My belief is our children have unique gifts, and we need to look out for them. The way to help a child grow with confidence and

Letting them know you care is like investing in a savings account, the more you put in the more you'll get out!

for them to unfold and emerge is with acknowledgment, kindness and an awareness of what we say and how we say it.

When Eden was little and achieved something, I would tell him it was wonderful and so was he. My mum, a staunch Catholic, would say "You shouldn't say that to him, you'll make him big headed." Different opinions for different times.

My mother was an excellent seamstress and would often make my sister and I dresses. As my sister and I were going to bed, mum would often get the paper dress-making pattern out. I always loved watching her unfold the thin tissue paper with lines on it for all the different parts of the dress, and unfold material to lay it flat on the table to place these paper pieces on, then pin them before cutting them out.

In the morning there would be two identical dresses for my sister and I, one smaller for my sister and one larger for me. I remember one particular day coming down and seeing the dresses she had made. I can see them clearly, the floral print and lace collar, with a bow made from tubular ribbon of the same material as the dress. I would love to watch mum make these ribbons, using a pencil to turn the thin stitched piece of material inside out. I put the dress on. I loved it, I had hold of the bottom of the dress at the sides as I twirled round, very happy, and was shocked when my mum pointed her finger at me and said sternly "And don't you dare think you look pretty in that dress. That's vanity and vanity is a sin." Well that took the wind out of my sails.

I know now she was doing her best. She didn't want me being sinful and was warning me away from that. We were always told not to brag or think we were good at things, which really puzzled me. If God made me, then I'm only praising him (I was taught to believe it was a man in the sky), surely he knew what he was doing and had got it right? By celebrating me wasn't I just celebrating God? It was confusing as a child, just as funerals were when I was little. If the person who had died had gone to heaven, a place that we were all aiming for, then why were so many people crying and upset? Life can be confusing for children. We don't always explain things well. We may leave out crucial bits of information… like the size of gorillas! I'll explain.

I watched the film King Kong when I was child and was very sad when he was killed at the end, though I was frightened by him too, the size of him. I said to my mother after seeing it, "There aren't really such things as gorillas though are there?" "Yes of course there are", she told me. "Not near us though?" I asked, hoping for reassurance there weren't. "Oh yes", she said, "at Belle Vue Zoo", which was very close to where we lived. I didn't sleep well for a long time, worried they might escape and stomp on our house. She didn't remember to add that they weren't as big as King Kong!

Encourage your children to use their imagination

"What the mind can conceive and believe, it can achieve"
Napoleon Hill

One of the things that happens to children is that they are encouraged to stop day-dreaming and using their imagination in a lot of cases. They are often told to be realistic and their dreams are shattered. We can belittle their dreams or ambitions. When they want to do something, encourage it. Let them live in their imagination. When we keep focusing on something we truly want to achieve and believe we can do it, we can achieve it. If your child wants to be a premier footballer or a famous singer let them aim for that. Remember if one person can, if it's possible for other people to do this, then it can be possible for your child too.

Shakespeare wrote in *Twelfth Night* "If music be the food of love, play on", so if your child loves music let them "play on", encourage them, share it with them, discuss it, introduce new music, artists. Music, the arts, crafts, all creative pursuits are necessary ingredients, I believe, for a well-balanced childhood. We sometimes neglect this area for academia and it is just as important. In fact, some children are far better at these right-brained activities than they are at left-brained ones such as those taught in school (see Part 3 Chapter 4, Know your child's learning style). A book for children exploring the power of the imagination is *The Power of Henry's Imagination* from the same team that brought us *The Secret, The Power, The Magic* and *Hero*.[3] Join in with their wonderment, be more child-like with them, play more. Really see and take note of the wonder in everyday things that we take for granted. Water in the tap, that we have electricity, the way the kettle, hoover, toaster work. That someone invented an umbrella, shoes, radio, TV, internet, car... so many things. Acknowledge them and encourage your children to as well. Be aware and grateful for nature, the petals of a flower, the colours in birds' wings, the multi-coloured leaves on the trees, or the ground on your walk to school. Stop and appreciate them and let your child do the same. Children have a sense of wonder and awe in nature and in manufactured things, how

Amplify their aptitude.

Remember the five "E"s: Explore, Experiment, Experience, Express and Enjoy.

---

[3] Skye Byrne *The Power of Henry's Imagination* (Simon & Schuster Children's UK 2015).

things work. They love to explore, so it's a shame that all too often we're in a hurry, have to get on, haven't got time for it. Enjoy this time when our children want to share and have fun, it's to be celebrated, it doesn't last. We get our priorities mixed up and it's over all too soon. Remember, children are here to Explore, Experiment, Experience, Express and Enjoy life.

> "There are only two ways to live your life. One is as though nothing is a miracle. The other is as though everything is a miracle."
>
> Albert Einstein

Ideas to expand their imagination

Using the imagination is especially helpful in school holidays and when they are stuck inside, not able to go out. We can use our imagination to create whatever we want, wherever we want, even for younger children. On a routine car journey or the way to school, ask where they are going today and come up with as many different places as you can. You suggest and let their imagination run wild.

- To Africa on a safari, what different animals might you encounter?
- To the South Pole to live in an igloo, what might you see and do there?
- Into space in a rocket ship, passing stars and galaxies, what else might you see?
- To Venice on a gondola, eating ice cream and singing opera.
- To America, visiting the Statue of Liberty, going inside and climbing up to the top.

You can do this kind of thing indoors, building trains, planes, boats, rocket ships, UFOs out of anything you have, or igloos, tents, wigwams and caves with no more than a sheet over chairs. You need only provide the basic items and their imagination will do the rest.

Rather than restrict them, encourage them. Let them blossom. This use of imagination is good for the brain, it fires neurons off that help create ways of thinking and habits that are beneficial to them in all areas of learning and life.

Look at the word imagination. I-magi-nation. We are a nation of magi (magicians) with I (that's you) at the start of it.

I know when I was at school if a child was gazing out of the window, daydreaming and possibly not listening, they were likely to have a board duster or chalk thrown at them. I'm sure this wouldn't happen today (not allowed!) and I think board dusters are a thing of the past. What's interesting is while that child was thinking about something else, using their imagination (as long as it was in a positive way) that was actually useful, nothing at all wrong with having dreams and aspirations. It could possibly be more beneficial than listening to calculus, or algebra, or whatever the lesson was, if that was something the child would never use. I'm not saying learning isn't important, of course it is, just there needs to be a good balance of encouraging imagination, dreams, hopes, goals and not keeping education solely academic. (Though do remember what we said earlier about balance in Oxygen Mask Thinking.) Another interesting fact is that very often, when that child was asked what the teacher had just said, they knew! That's a bit like when we drive somewhere and suddenly find ourselves at our destination, without actually really remembering driving there, or being on public transport and suddenly arriving at our stop. Our mind has been somewhere else, or part of our mind has, though enough of us was still present to be aware at some level and stay safe. This is because we operate at both a conscious and unconscious (or subconscious) level all the time.

Stop blaming them

We often blame our children for how we feel. When we no longer say "you" make me mad, or upset or angry, or whatever emotion it is we're feeling (choosing to allow in our body), we are caring for them and not causing them to feel bad, sad or guilty.

April 2006 was the beginning of what has been and continues to be an incredible journey for me in personal and spiritual development. It was the second day of my Neuro Linguistic Programming (NLP) course. I was sitting in a training room somewhere in Haslemere, Surrey when I was introduced to Meta Models, a system of looking at language. These models are used to recognize what thoughts and beliefs lie underneath what's actually being said. The trainer explained cause and effect where cause is incorrectly placed outside oneself, for example when someone says "You make me angry, or sad, or upset", and went on to say "nobody else can *make* you anything, you allow yourself to be those things". I was shocked. It was as though I'd literally been electrocuted or at least put my tongue on a 9v battery, the rectangular ones used in many smoke alarms (yes we often did that as children, daring each other to!). It stopped me in my tracks and the reality of it, the absolute obviousness of it, hit me hard and the thought "Oh my God, I've been blaming my boys for so much for so long and it isn't them, it's me!" ran through my head. I knew then I was the one who had to change how I thought and behaved. I'd had a fridge magnet with the

Gandhi quote: "We must be the change we want to see in the world." For years I thought I got it, I didn't until then!

Take control – of you!

I learnt that I had personal power and choice. That no one else made me anything. Nobody else made me mad, angry or upset. I allowed myself to experience those emotions, those feelings. If I blamed somebody else then I had given my personal power away. This doesn't mean I didn't feel emotions of anger or disappointment or sadness sometimes. What I would do is stay calm. Not react and blame, lash out or shout. I would go inside and identify what I was actually feeling, where was it in my body, how big it felt. Really analyse the actual feeling I could feel in my body. Then start to let it go. Remembering it was my body, I was in control of it. I would really identify with the feeling so I could imagine it as whatever it seemed to come up as, a stone or a brick perhaps, or cloudy liquid, and worked on letting it go, so in my imagination it started to dissipate and I could feel it leaving my body. This was my take on The Sedona Method. Now I have found The Energy Alignment Method (EAM) and trained as a facilitator and mentor. I explain more a little further on. EAM has been for me the most effective transformational energy psychology tool for releasing anything unwanted and unhelpful. Thoughts, beliefs, habits, anything that isn't serving me and being able to align to a positive, higher vibrational state and being happier, calmer, more in control in all areas of life.

Realizing I *allowed* myself to feel whatever it was I was feeling and no one was *making* me, no arm twisting, no control over me, always my choice, put me firmly on the cause side of the equation, not the effect side. If I chose to believe someone else was to blame for the way I felt, I was being a victim. I learnt that I am responsible for what I experience and I choose what I feel. It took a bit of getting used to this idea and I know a lot of people struggle with this and that's why I think the following story I'm going to relate is amazing.

It was a beautiful March morning and my youngest son, Eden, and I decided to walk to the shop, he was in a good mood, commenting on the beautiful blue sky, the trees and saying what a lovely place we lived in. He's an amazing young man and I love the way he notices and appreciates things a lot. I decided to ask him a question. "On a scale of 1–10, Eden, how good is your relationship with your parents?" "About an 8 or 9", he replied, which I think is fantastic and I told him that. Then I asked him "What would make it a 10?" What he said next blew me away, and I am quoting his exact words: "What I could do differently."

Wow, talk about responsibility! I asked him to explain and he told me it was only when he got angry with something or upset and then got in a bad mood that it wasn't so good. I told him that it was incredible that he was not blaming anyone else and taking responsibility for what he was experiencing. He had grasped the idea of personal power a lot earlier than I did! We are powerful creative beings and don't use our potential as much as we could. We are incredibly complicated multicellular organisms, let's explore that further in the next chapter.

When you point a finger, remember three are pointing back at you.

Part 2

Energetic beings

Chapter 3

Who and what we really are

In 2006 I went on an NLP course, as I have previously mentioned. I learnt hypnotherapy and was introduced to *The Secret* by Rhonda Byrne. This is where I was introduced to the "law of attraction" and the idea that everything is energy. I'm sure I'd heard it at school in science at some point, though not really grasped what it meant.

Everything is energy, including us. Nothing is solid in the universe, even though it may look that way. We're not. Look down at one of your hands and see a solid, fairly still hand and then imagine the other one under a microscope. You know they won't look the same, the one under the microscope won't show you what you see with limited human sight; it will show you moving, vibrating energy. Which is real? They both are. We just can't see what's under the microscope normally.

The quantum soup of us all

This term "quantum soup" is a phrase a very good friend of mine doesn't like at all and she likes even less the concept of it. She doesn't want to be mixed up with everyone else in this quantum soup. Well like it or not she is, we all are!

We are living in a dual world. One of energy that is vibrating and never still; it has no edges, nothing starts and finishes, it is all connected. We are all, on the energetic level, connected. The edge of our visible body isn't really where we stop, our energetic field is emitted and goes on and on and we have what is referred to as our aura, the distinctive atmospheric quality that can be felt and measured. We are constantly sending out an electromagnetic field, which has a frequency, a vibration and carries information. It can be measured for about 20 feet from our bodies by apparatus called a SQUID, a Sequential Quantum Interference Decoder. We communicate with this, send out messages and signals that attract back things of the same frequency and vibration. The law of vibration and the law of attraction are two of the universal laws as indisputable as the law of gravity.

Feel it for yourself by rubbing your hands together, as if warming them, do it for several seconds, then stop. Concentrate on your hands, feel the tingle in them, in your fingers. If you don't feel much at first, rub them again and concentrate on the feeling. Then slowly move your hands apart an inch or so, then push them together, move your hands in and out to feel the energy field between your hands. Then concentrate on the rest of your body, starting at the feet, can you feel any tingling there, up your shins or back of your legs, arms, back, top of your head? Think about how you are always vibrating and when we are able to raise the frequency of our body, have it vibrating at a high level, energy free flowing, we then attract more of that high energy back to us. Our thoughts, beliefs and emotions all have an energetic vibration and output. The energy we give off can be felt and read by others, especially our children. They often know what's going on with us; if something's wrong they will feel it and we don't have to say anything. When I was depressed and on Prozac and not in a good place at all after my divorce, my youngest son, Eden, would often ask me "What's wrong, Mum?" when I hadn't said a thing!

Emotions – energy in motion

Energy is everywhere and everything. It is constantly present. It has a frequency, it vibrates. Our emotions are energy in motion, they have a frequency and vibration. We know this when we experience them, we can feel them in us. You've experienced, I imagine, that feeling of rage or anger in you, or sadness, grief? And on the flip side, love, excitement, peace, joy? We feel it. Our thoughts are energy too, they have an electromagnetic quality. Our thoughts and beliefs, anything we experience in our body, has an effect on the make-up of the body. When a woman is pregnant, carrying a baby, then that baby experiences the frequency of her emotions, thoughts and beliefs. Because energy can't be created or destroyed and is simply re-cycled, changes form, then energy from the past, wherever it has been, whatever it has been before, then becomes present in that baby, that foetus and repeats whatever that energy has been before. It brings with it knowledge, beliefs or patterns of behaviour that have previously existed. What happens in the womb affects the baby and can affect the child growing up and also in adulthood. EAM (see below) is the modality I use myself and with clients to release negative emotions, states, beliefs, thoughts and habits.

I know that I and other women I have worked with have experienced and had negative emotions, thoughts, worries or beliefs during pregnancy, some of which have been passed on, handed down and instilled by default into the child. This can manifest in the quality of the relationship with their child. They may not consciously know this or what they have carried and yet are having a difficult time with their child. Their child really pushes their buttons, they are annoyed or frustrated or irritated with them (or with one child more than another) and they don't really know why. Then when using EAM and the emotional scale (a list of emotions starting with the lowest vibrational frequency to the highest) we identify they have perhaps resentment, guilt, shame, frustration, anger, fear, powerlessness and the vibration of that is affecting their relationship. We can then release the energy of this.

When I was carrying my third child and discovered I was having a third boy and not the girl we had wanted, I was very disappointed and perhaps a little angry. I was definitely sad and those feelings would have been affecting my baby. They were negative emotions and negative, low vibrational frequency has resistant energy, not high vibrational positive, flowing energy and this causes the cells of the body (the baby's too) to not function optimally. Luckily I didn't stay in that state for long. At each stage of pregnancy the foetus is developing and different parts of the body are developing that are affected by the environment, which of course is the mother and all that is going on in her womb, in her. It has been claimed that if very negative emotions are being experienced by the mother, for a sustained period, at the time a particular organ or part of the body is being formed then the quality of that body part in the foetus is affected, inhibited in being the best it can be due to the quality of the energy in its environment. I have used EAM to identify and release any negative emotions I had during pregnancy (and afterwards) with all my boys and was surprised at some I had that I consciously wouldn't have thought I was carrying, though they were present in my energy and at an unconscious level.

I want to help eliminate fear in parents and any negative emotions that arise, any limiting beliefs that are not serving you or your children or any generational patterns and ways of thinking and behaving that have been passed down, whether at a conscious or unconscious level. I use

EAM with parents and want you to be able to use this energy method for releasing negativity and replace it with empowering positivity. This means releasing the energetic frequency and replacing with a higher energetic vibration, setting yourself and your children free.

An introduction to the Energy Alignment Method

The Energy Alignment Method (EAM) was created by Yvette Taylor, who has inspired and supported me on my journey and to whom I am very grateful, and always will be, for being my mentor and training me in EAM to become one of the first accredited EAM Mentors in the world. It is a certified and recognized therapy by The International Institute for Complimentary Therapy.

In Yvette's *The Ultimate Self-Help Book* she explains "EAM is founded in years of working in energy medicine, the Law of Attraction and traditional Chinese medicine. Its methods include elements of kinesiology, neuroscience research, NLP, Positive Psychology and Eastern spiritual principles. The magic of EAM is that it enables you to shift energy." I have experienced this to be true.

How to use EAM

Stand with your feet hip width apart, have your knees soft (not locked), be relaxed, arms and hands loosely by your sides. Ask simple yes or no questions. Your body will usually sway forward for a yes answer and backward for a no. If it's the other way round we have an energy reversal, explained below.

If you feel no movement, there are many different reasons for this, as your sway is affected by different sources in your environment. Below is a list of what may be affecting your sway.

- Being tired
- Being on medication
- Alcohol
- Sugar
- Caffeine
- Foods in your diet
- Computers and other technology
- Being exposed to electromagnetic fields (EMFs)
- Cleansing, hygiene products and perfumes
- Particular environments
- Other people (their energy or what you are feeling or thinking about them)

You can ask whether any of these are affecting you, though if they are you will not get a true answer as you may have no or little movement or an energy reversal and have to deal with releasing the energy reversal first.

Dr David Hawkins discusses the use of kinesiology techniques alongside his map of consciousness and explains that people operating at a low frequency, having a low vibration (below 200 on the scale) are in survival mode and in a reversed energy state, not in flow or of a high vibration and may have little or no movement.[1] This can be addressed with EAM, releasing energy reversals and resistance energy. This is more complicated to do alone and working with a mentor is highly recommended.

---

[1] David R. Hawkins *Power vs. Force: The Hidden Determinants of Human Behaviour* (Hay House 2002).

I want to introduce the method I use with people and if you wish to know more you can, of course, investigate EAM further. The following is the handout sheet issued to mentors and people on any EAM programme.

The five steps to the Energy Alignment Method

Now you know your YES and NO, you can ask your body simple yes/no questions. Think about something that may have been troubling you. Stand with feet hip width apart, close your eyes and relax your knees.

Step 1 – You ask

This step is to give you clarity on what you need to shift. Ask your energy a simple question about the subject or situation to see if that's what you need to work on.

Example: "Am I holding on to resistance or worry when I think about my child going to school?"

Step 2 – You move

Your energy body will respond and give you the YES or NO response to the question you've asked. Forward is usually YES and backward is usually NO. If anything else, check for energy reversal. If YES go to Step 3. If NO and you feel in flow go to Step 5.

Step 3 – You experience

This step is about assessing what is happening in your energy when you think about that subject. There are three ways you can do this step. Choose which is appropriate for you.

- How do you feel?

    Describe what it feels like in your body. What size, colour or shape is it? Where is it? Is it moving, or still, heavy or light? What does it feel like?
    How many of them?
    Using the sway find the specific number of resistances, e.g. "Do I have more than 100?" (sway will say yes or no). If NO, then ask "Do I have more than 50?" If NO, then ask "Do I have more than 25?" If YES, then ask "Do I have more than 30?" If NO, ask a number between 25 and 30. You don't always have to have a specific number but you get the idea.
    How does it look in your mind?
    When you close your eyes and think about it, your resistance or challenge, do you see a picture, an image? Describe what is happening in the picture.

Step 4 – You transform

Now you are clear what it feels like in your body, how many there are or what the picture looks like you can do the release statement. Use these words: "I am ready to release (whatever the subject is, or this number of resistances or this image, picture or feeling and describe it). I release it from my energy in all forms, on all levels, at all points in time."

Repeat this statement at least three times or until you can no longer feel it. You may have to do this another two or three times. Check in with the sway and ask. When released you can go to Step 5.

Examples of release statements:

Feelings

"I am ready to release this hard red circle in my stomach when I think about my child going to school, I release it from my energy, in all forms, on all levels, at all points in time."

Numbers

"I am ready to release these 534 thoughts and beliefs about my child going to school. I release them from my energy, in all forms, on all levels, at all points in time."

Images

"I am ready to release this image of a brick wall (or whatever it is). I release it from my energy, in all forms, on all levels, at all points in time."

Repeat Step 4 until you have released the resistance around it.

Ask the sway "Have I released this resistance around...?"

When YES, then move on to Step 5. If NO and you have used the statement several times, it could be something else. Reword or rethink what else it could be.

Step 5 – You manifest

This time you get to choose what you experience. This is where you manifest your new future. Now you are ready to allow a new feeling, belief, thought or pattern.

Choose a positive, affirmative statement.

"I am ready to receive/create/feel/manifest/experience (whatever it is you want). I allow this into my energy in all forms, on all levels, at all points in time." Repeat this three times until your body responds with a positive forward YES. Keep repeating until you feel it in your energy.

Examples of allowing statements:

Feeling

"I am ready to allow this big soft circle of calm confidence into my body when I think about my child going to school. I allow this into my energy in all forms, on all levels, at all points in time."

Numbers

"I am ready to allow myself to have 100,000 new positive beliefs that I am always calm and can cope with situations really well. I allow this into my energy in all forms, on all levels, at all points in time."

Images

"I am ready to allow this bright new pathway to take me forward. I allow this into my energy in all forms, on all levels, at all points in time."

How to deal with an energy reversal

You know there is an energy reversal when one of the following happens:

1. Back to front sway. You get a backward sway for something that should be yes and forward for a no.
2. Side to side. You sway side to side or go round in circles, telling you something else is going on.
3. Step 4 not shifting. You've done Step 4 several times and still not shifted something.
4. The emotion is intense. The emotion is overwhelming or you feel stuck, frozen.

For now keep it simple and find out what age you were when you created this energy reversal. Ask "How old was I when I created this energy reversal about or around (whatever it is)."

Use the sway to find out. "Was I under X?" and then use the sway the same way as you did to find numbers of resistances.

You can ask "Was this about…?", e.g. it may be something you are aware of that happened at that age, a certain situation or involving certain people.

"I am ready to release this energy reversal about… from the age of… I release it from my energy in all forms, on all levels, at all points in time."

You may need to repeat two or three times.

Ask the sway "Have I released this energy reversal about…?"

If you've released it move on to Step 5. If not there are many other ways of exploring what's going on, with help. An EAM Mentor is recommended.

Have fun with it, explore the possibilities. Energy is limitless and so are you.

A common erroneous belief

The most common belief I have encountered with parents is they believe they are 100% responsible for their children. Of course, there is a responsibility to keep them safe and do our best for them. We are not responsible for all their choices, though. That is their responsibility. They learn best from experience. I won't even say mistakes as I don't believe there are any. Everything experienced teaches something, there is learning in it, a lesson, and our children will learn best for themselves, not because we told them so.

One parent I worked with, when we first met, believed she was responsible for her daughter, who was eighteen, who already had a child and was pregnant again. She thought she needed to do everything, or as much as she could possibly do for her daughter and grandchildren, because this was her responsibility. It's admirable and fine to want to help, just not to take on all, or too much, responsibility and it's erroneous to think and believe we have to or should do.

Her sway confirmed yes (forward) to her thinking and believing that she was responsible for her daughter and her choices. This wasn't helpful, it was a belief based in fear and worry and had negative emotions and therefore negative energy around it. Using EAM we released her worry, fear, anxiety and concern and aligned her to feeling calm and accepting the situation, believing it was as it was meant to be and that everything happens for a reason. We then asked the question "Are you 100% responsible for your daughter?" and she got a no sway (backward). We then had tears, which are always good, it's a release, and she was now energetically in flow and aligned to her truth. Still able to choose what she did to help without the energy of fear-based emotions, worry, anxiety or guilt. Remember Kahlil Gibran:

Your children are not your children
They are the sons and daughters of Life's longing for itself.
They come through you but not from you,
And though they are with you yet they belong not to you[2]

We can use EAM with children too. They are very good at being able to tell you what they are feeling, even if they can't name it. Avoid naming and labelling as much as possible, as we can put ideas into their head and they then take on board they have that, feel it and are it, which isn't always helpful, e.g. labelling your child as anxious or shy or saying and letting them hear "Oh they're not good in new situations" or "They find (whatever it is) difficult, hard". This encourages them to believe it. Often people say "I am" rather than "I have" some condition e.g., dyslexia, diabetes, or say I am angry, sad, disappointed etc., these are emotions and temporary, you are not them, you have them. If someone tells me they are dyslexic, or anything else, I ask "And what else are you more than that?" It causes them to think and reframe, they are more than that, they just have that. I have a little finger; I wouldn't say I am a little finger.

Children have great and vivid imaginations and can tell you how what they are feeling looks, what colour it is, what shape, what it's made of etc., and then we release it using the releasing statement three times and then ask what they would like instead and allow that in at Step 5. One eight year old who was experiencing bullying at school said it felt like a piece of heavy green wood from shoulder to shoulder at the front and at the back. She showed me the shape of it and we released it and allowed in a warm, fuzzy, squidgy, sparkly, round, soft yellow sun thing.

---

[2] Gibran *The Prophet*.

Raise yourself to raise your child

A lot of us are still carrying childhood wounds and our inner child is hurting. Until we heal ourselves and are whole, we still have growing up to do. If we haven't grown up properly, how are we able to help our child grow up? To raise our child well, we have to raise ourselves first. I mean our vibration.

How do you start your day, what's the very first thing you think, when you wake up? Is it negative or positive? Do you groan and think "Oh no, I've got to get up, I need to get the kids up"? "I have to get ready for work"? These are not high vibrational thoughts, nor are they true (see Part 4 Chapter 6, How we lie to ourselves). Start your day with an attitude of gratitude. It's a great way to start the day and we really do have a lot to be grateful for. I know the old me would often wake up when I heard a neighbour starting their car at 4:30am and be really annoyed, "Grrrr, for God's sake", I would think, pulling the pillow over my ears to block out the sound. I might wake up and the boys were already in the kitchen burning toast! Again, "For God's sake", very short-tempered and not tolerant. I learnt to turn these things into things to be grateful for. If I could hear my neighbour staring his car, I had the gift of hearing. I was grateful for that and the fact I wasn't getting up at that time to go to work. The fact I could smell burnt toast, meant I had a sense of smell, for which I was very grateful, I could also smell other lovely smells too. Some people can't smell. It also meant I had food in for my boys, I had my boys, they were up and I wasn't going to have to struggle getting them out of bed. When we stop and think, before reacting (often over-reacting) and looking at a situation we get chance to think "What else does this mean that's good and positive?" It doesn't take long and when you get used to doing this, it becomes second nature, to find the gratitude, see what's good about it and wear rose coloured specs more often (see Part 2 Chapter 3, Wear rose coloured specs).

If you don't already, start writing a gratitude journal. I write in the morning. I usually start with being alive. If I've woken up and know I'm here that's a good start. That might sound a little flippant, or you might say you're not particularly grateful for waking up! Think of the implications of if you hadn't, again, just for a minute, to help you feel grateful. If you hadn't woken, who would have found you, what would happen to your children, partner (if you have one), family? How would people feel? Think of all you'd miss in your children's lives if you weren't here! No dwelling on this, just another point of view to consider. Remember to use your *Parenting Magic* journal too (see pp. 189–191).

I list lots of things that occur to me to be grateful for. That I have a bed to sleep on, nice clean covers, a carpet on my floor to step on to out of my bed, slippers, my dressing gown, a bathroom, flushing toilet, clean running water. Electricity to turn the lights on, kettle, heating etc., it's a huge list and yours could be too. We take so much for granted and don't take the time to really appreciate it. Start to do that. Appreciate and develop your attitude of gratitude. This generates positive feelings and energy and we feel better. We are body bags of energy and vibrate at a certain frequency. The higher the vibration or the frequency, then the better, healthier and happier we feel and are and this energy affects and influences our children.

Intention setting

The other thing we tend to do is let the day happen to us, as though we have no control. We may not be able to alter all events, situations or circumstances we encounter, but what we can do is alter our attitude to and about these things. We can step into our personal power and choose how we are going to respond. The day doesn't happen to us, it happens through us, Michael Beckwith says, through us and for us, not to us, and what we experience is a reflection of our perspective and energy, i.e. the vibrational frequency we emit.[3] Decide how your day will be, how you are going to feel and be.

Consciously decide how or what you intend your day to be like, how you intend to be and throughout the day remind yourself. Michael Beckwith talks about there being an intention deficit rather than an attention deficit! Choose simple intentions and instructions, like "Today I am going to be happy" or patient, tolerant, understanding, calm, peaceful or helpful. Smile at people, do one random act of kindness, have fun, laugh often. You choose. Get into the habit of intention setting, not just for your day for your life, and empower your children to do the same. Many people just go through life letting it happen to them, without a clear picture, or vision, of what exactly they want it to look like, be like or feel like. Your life is a blank canvas and you get to paint whatever picture you like. Choose a masterpiece, you're the artist. Teach this to your children too. In fact, when it becomes natural and consistent for you to do this and your children see it, it will be natural for them.

---

[3] Michael Bernard Beckwith *The Answer is You: Waking Up to Your Full Potential* (Sounds True 2009).

Segment intend

Our day is broken up into different segments, different activities, and when one ends, like finishing work, that's the end of that segment and the next one is your journey home. We can intentionally send out the energy of the thoughts we're having, or the way we feel and that influences what we will then experience. I learnt this from Esther Hicks in *Ask and it is Given*.[4]

You are a human being not a human doing.

I used to drive home from work knowing the boys would be home from school or college, thinking, I bet they'll be arguing when I get in, they won't have even thought about starting tea, bet they haven't emptied the dishwasher, or brought the washing in, and so on. All negative thoughts and expectations and guess what? I was right. So I started to change my thoughts and self-talk, to the boys will be playing on a game together, or watching a DVD and laughing having a good time, they'll have tidied up, emptied the dishwasher, so I was in a better state when I arrived home. It wasn't an instant fix though this, along with other tools and techniques I am sharing with you, started to make the difference. What they all have in common is that I was the one making the change.

---

[4] Esther Hicks and Jerry Hicks *Ask and it is Given: Learning to Manifest Your Desires* (Hay House second edition 2004).

To Be or not to Be, that is the question

Are you spending more time Doing than Being? We can get so caught up in day to day things, the mundane, routine and necessary practical issues of the day that we miss it. It's over in the blink of an eye and we haven't taken time to enjoy it, have fun, smile, laugh, do a good deed. We just get on with it. An interesting question people often ask children is "What do you want to be when you grow up?" and usually when they ask they mean, what do you want to do, what job or career do you want? Surely the best thing they can want to be is happy, healthy, in love, content, successful, fulfilled.

Often people have a to-do list and see their day, life even, as a series of events and things to do. Well, remember you are a human *being*… not a human *doing*. Have a to-be list as well as a to-do list.

Every time you write down what you have to do, write down what or how you're going to be. Your list might be a bit like the one below: make sure there are as many things on your to-be list as there are on your to-do list.

To Do
Take kids to school
Go to post office
Get food shopping
(and buy birthday present for…)
Pick up from dry cleaners
Make phone call to…

To Be
Grateful
Calm
Kind
Helpful
Patient
Tolerant
Smiley!

Choose positive states of being that you can consciously think about and intend to be them. We do have so much to be grateful for. Remember even when your children are challenging and you're having a bad day, there are people who would love to have children and can't, or people who have lost their children. I'm not encouraging you to dwell on the negative side, just a quick reminder of this truth and then be grateful for having your children.

Be present

Remember you are a human being, so take time to be and enjoy it. It is hard to think that the time goes so quickly, it does and it's important to make the most of now in the best way possible. When we are experiencing a tough time, remember "This too shall pass", everything does! Eckhart Tolle's book *The Power of Now* helps us to understand and appreciate exactly what the title says… the power of now.[5]

There is only ever "now" that's all we can ever really experience: the past is memory, the future, imagination. I wrote this poem for my eldest son, Kris, when he was four years old (over thirty-six years ago now!):

---

[5] Eckhart Tolle *The Power of Now: A Guide to Spiritual Enlightenment* (Yellow Kite 2020).

There is only now. There is only ever "this" now.
This green, that blue. These wonderful feelings
because of you.
Your laugh is precious, don't ever stop.
Your pleasure, simple, you don't ask a lot.
I wish this time, these feelings, this experience
would never end.
My very special person, not even five years old yet.
My very special friend.

The best present you can give your child is be it!

(I wrote this long before I understood the implication of using "don't"! See Part 3 Chapter 4, Ditch your "don'ts".)

When we are caught up in the hustle and bustle of life, on that hamster wheel, it's hard to think that this time with our children goes by so quickly. It does and it's so important to make the most and the best of this now. I look back at when I was bringing the boys up single-handed and thinking "I'll always be taking them to school". I'm not, that's passed, as everything does. It changes, nothing stays the same, the only consistent thing is change. It's a good thing to say to yourself, when things are a bit tough, "This too shall pass". Whatever it is, it will.

"Change is the only constant in life"

Heraclitus, Greek philosopher

Another saying I like is "the only thing that's really predictable is unpredictability". Good to remember when things don't work out as you planned or expected!

Positivity

I love Michael Beckwith (mentioned earlier), he has so many wonderful sayings. I like his idea of waking up and having a cup of "Positivi –TEA".[6] Do this and wear rose coloured specs.

Wear rose coloured specs

Always find the good in any situation. Every cloud has a silver lining. Even though it may not, at first, be very apparent. Sometimes we have to wait for hindsight so we can look back and realize that whatever it was that happened that we didn't think was a good thing, actually was because if it hadn't happened we wouldn't be where we are now. So let's have hindsight in the now (obviously foresight!) in the present and re-think a situation. When I was looking for a car for my youngest son after he had passed his driving test, my sister had just sold her car at a very reasonable price. I was annoyed for a while because we'd missed such a great bargain. Eden hadn't told anyone he was taking his test so it was a surprise and when he passed and I wanted to buy a car, I had just missed my sister's! We then found one online we liked and as we couldn't go to see that until the next day, we missed that one too. Another Arghh! Then, through an unexpected set of circumstances, we were offered one that suited Eden better and the price for the car was much less than the others. In fact, the car and the insurance cost the same as I would have paid for my sister's car. Though for a while I was annoyed and kept dwelling on missing it, with the "If only…" thought, the universe knew what she was doing. Already had a plan, we just didn't know.

The benefits of wearing rose coloured specs

- You will start to notice the things your children do right.

---

[6] Beckwith *The Answer is You.*

- When you also tell them these things, they'll start to respond differently to what you say.
- You'll start to learn to appreciate what's unique and special about them. Every child has their own gift, they just unwrap them at different times.
- You'll realize some things you viewed as negative are really positive, like the strength of character they build by learning from doing things their way.

Dr Milton Erikson (considered the father of hypnotherapy and a family psychiatrist and psychologist, 1901–1980) had a couple bring their troublesome daughter to him. They were struggling with her being strong-willed, awkward, not doing as she was told, and he said and isn't that a good thing, she knows her own mind and is less likely to be influenced by peers and talked into doing things she doesn't want, or something very similar. He wore rose coloured specs and had the ability to *reframe* situations.

Ten top tips to get into the habit of wearing rose coloured specs

1. Stop reacting and learn to respond. Take a deep breath before responding to any situation, incident or something that's been said.
2. Find something good about what has happened, even if it's only: "It could have been worse."
3. Learn to think outside the box, expand your mind. What could, will or might happen, or is possible now, because of what has taken place?
4. Set a great example to your children of how to deal with situations in the best way. By doing this, you're teaching them acceptance.
5. Remember your children will do as you do.

6. Behave in the way you want your child to, be a good role model.
7. Read Edward de Bono's books *Lateral Thinking* and *Six Thinking Hats* for new ideas. Many brain teasers and electronic games also give you different perspectives. The brain is incredibly malleable and can be re-wired at any age. We are using so little of our brain's (and mind's) capacity.[7]
8. Practice doing simple tasks differently, like folding your arms the opposite way or putting your hands together linking fingers, notice which thumb is on top then do it the other way! Brush your teeth, sweep, hoover, clean worktops with the opposite hand to the one you usually use. This highlights there is always another way to do things.
9. Be grateful for what you've got instead of looking at what you haven't got.
10. Practise gratitude for all the good things having your children brings you, and you might want to tell them occasionally too!

One of the first times I put this into practice was when I decided to look at my son's habit of leaving rubbish in his pockets in a different way. Something that drove me mad when putting his clothes in the washing machine was the amount of rubbish he had left in his pockets. I'd then have to empty them so I wouldn't have a broken machine. It would range from crisp packets and chocolate wrappers to broken pens, coins, bus tickets, wheels of toy cars, lolly sticks. All sorts. I really had to think "What's good about this?" I finally decided that it was that he actually brought his rubbish home and didn't litter the streets.

---

[7] Edward de Bono *Lateral Thinking: A Textbook of Creativity* (Penguin Life 2016) and *Six Thinking Hats* (Penguin 2000).

Wear rose coloured specs to see silver linings.

When we surrender to what's happening and consider our response, we become responsible (response-able). I encourage us to always wear rose coloured specs. Always look for what's good in a situation, even if it's only "It could have been worse." There usually is a worse-case scenario, though I also accept there are occasions where it doesn't feel that's possible. Even then, whatever has happened means that something else will happen or be possible because of it.

Part 3

Communication

This chapter will cover the full extent of what communication is. We are all communicating all the time, sometimes well and positively and at other times, not so! We can't not communicate. Whether it's through our energy and the vibration of, as we have already discussed, or words (that have a vibration and frequency as well as meaning), or our actions, behaviours and habits. They all say something about us and that's what we are emitting and communicating.

Chapter 4

The definition of communication

The definition of communication according to the *Oxford English Dictionary* is "the exchanging or imparting of knowledge by speaking, writing, or some other medium".[1] I want to look at all the ways we communicate with our children, our words, language and the "some other medium" that is us, our body. It emits an electromagnetic energy that has a frequency felt by our children. Our thoughts are energy; when we have a thought, neurons are fired and an electrical current or signal is sent from one neuron to another across the synapse. The more often this particular thought or process happens, the easier the brain finds it to use the same pathway again in the future, our brain becomes wired to think this thought. We run the same thoughts over and over again and they become beliefs and then we act accordingly. Barbara Brennan, an American author (born 1939), has written extensively on the aura, this biofield, this energy body, and Rupert Sheldrake (born 1942), a British biologist and author, writes about the aura, or morphic field. Our unconscious programmes are very often unhelpful, untrue, negative and run limiting beliefs that we have unknowingly and we pass them on to our children through our energy.

---

[1] www.lexico.com/definition/communication [accessed April 2020].

I used to provide supported lodging for displaced teenagers. On one occasion I was about to have a young man come to stay with me. I was told that he didn't communicate much. He was in trouble with the police often, wouldn't stay in lessons and was fairly physical at school. That was him communicating loud and clear. His unhappiness, frustration, anger, sense of not belonging and the very fact he didn't particularly want to talk to or engage with adults spoke volumes. Whatever behaviour a child is exhibiting, there is always a good reason for it. It's important to look at what the underlying cause for the behaviour is, which we will do later in "Brain and child development".

Verbal communication

Language is defined as a "method of communication, either spoken or written, consisting of the use of words in a structured and conventional way".[2] A system of spoken or written symbols by means of which members of a certain social group or culture express themselves. There has to be an agreement at some point that the symbols mean something and that the way they are put together means something too.

I only speak, read and write in English (and know a little Spanish and French). In English we have 26 letters, only 26 and yet we can create thousands of words and order them in so many ways, we have thousands and thousands of books, stories and information. I often say in presentations or workshops I can say all the words in the English language that have ever been written, or ever will be written, in under five seconds. I'm usually challenged, or someone asks "How?" and I proceed to say the alphabet. Then say,

---

[2] www.lexico.com/en/definition/language [accessed April 2020].

all the words are there, just not necessarily in the right order (and if you're of a certain age, you may remember the late great comedian Eric Morecombe playing the piano tunelessly. When challenged by Ernie Wise, who says "You're playing all the wrong notes", Morecombe replies "I'm playing all the right notes, not necessarily in the right order." Exactly!) I'll then begin to write the alphabet out on a flip chart, just the first few letters. Then I take the letters b, e and d and ask what it says, people answer "bed" and immediately in their mind picture a bed, it's the way the mind works, it has an image stored that we retrieve. Then I will write c, g and e, or f, b and g and ask the same question. People can't say these letters together as a word, they have no point of reference for what it represents. So one combination of some of those 26 letters has meaning and another selection doesn't. It's because we have made an agreement to what their intrinsic meaning is. It's the meaning we have put on them. We have chosen and agreed, mass consciousness agrees on this. I then write in capital letters A B C and break down each letter into symbols, see the illustration below, and that's all the symbols we need. All the other letters can be made up from a combination and slight modification of these six symbols and oh my goodness the meaning we can create!

The importance of our spoken and written language

We have put the meaning to words. One word can mean different things to different people. I knew someone whose partner, when she suggested they did something, would say "I'd quite like to do that", she would then offer another suggestion, he might respond to that the same way "Yeah, I'd quite like that". It could go on a while. Until he asked her why she would ask him so many questions. It was because she interpreted "quite like to" as it being only an okay thing to do, whereas he meant he would *really* like that! The word "quite" meant something completely different to each of them. Our spoken language can be very confusing. As can written language: consider text messages or electronic message systems, missing the tone and body language means a lot can be misinterpreted!

Written words have so much power, they convey thoughts and intentions and have energy too. That's why journaling is so powerful, as are setting and writing down goals and intentions.

Think it and ink it into being

Thoughts become things. Everything we see, everything that exists first had to be a thought before it could become something. Whether that's an object or a behaviour, it has to first be thought.

This idea tied in beautifully with what I learnt from Esther and Jerry Hicks in *Ask and it is Given*.[3] I learnt about the

---

[3] Esther Hicks and Jerry Hicks *Ask and it is Given: Learning to Manifest Your Desires* (Hay House second edition 2004).

power of journaling from them, where you imagine how you want things to be and then write them as though they are that way now, using the present tense. Like goal setting, where we go out into the future and imagine something as we want it to be, as though we're experiencing it now. So when struggling with a relationship or a person, journal what you like or love about them and then expand and write it as you want it to be, i.e. make it up, even though it isn't that way yet, you are faking it till you make it. When we put out to the universe present tense statements, the universe catches up and says "Your wish is my command." I was having a challenging time with the boys in 2006 and found Hal, my middle son, most challenging. The one without the special needs and labels, though of course I realized that everything that had happened had affected him, his behaviours and how he felt about himself.

I wrote down how I wanted my relationship with Hal to be and wrote it as though it was now. First we pick a relationship that we would like to be better. Then we think about what we do like and love about that person. What we admire about them, something they do that we like. It might seem odd at first and even a little difficult; it gets easier. I decided I liked Hal when he was in a good mood and chatty, offering to make me a cup of tea and talk to me. I kept this image in my head and felt it, it is important to feel the good feeling, the vibration of that. I started to write "I love Hal when he is…" and then wrote as much as I could. Once I'd started, more positive things flowed. I loved his sense of humour, his ability to tell or recount a story or incident. How he was very eloquent and articulate, intelligent and caring. How he was excellent at cooking (without thinking of the mess he might leave in the process!). This helped highlight good points. I then wrote exactly what I wanted it to be like, still using present tense as though it already was, and I did this every day. Think it and ink it, works well. Positive thoughts, expressed on paper, put down in form, become so.

This, along with my whole new way of being in the now, being grateful and expressing it, looking for the good in situations, yielded the results I wanted. I saw the results of journaling and focusing on what I really wanted and started goal setting. Previously I knew I had had ambitions or dreams to do things in a vague and almost out-of-reach kind of way, pie in the sky ideas that were not really likely to come true. Now I was being encouraged to get clear on and be specific about what I wanted in life, write it down and set an intention for it to happen. I attended a Chris Howard personal development training in September 2007 and there wrote my first SMART goal, a goal that is Specific, Measured, Attainable, Realistic and Timed. You pick the date you want the goal to have happened by and really imagine it has happened, feel as though it has, see all you would see when it's happening, all you would hear and feel and smell, make it as lifelike as possible. This is a great tool and a good starting place, though I also now use Yvette Taylor's SMART acronym, where she means Specific, Manifest (by being in the right energetic space to allow it), Aligned (taking aligned positive action in the right vibration), Receive (be open and allow) and Trust (the universe and that it will happen).

Let's look at some ways to clearly communicate what we mean when we speak to our children.

Magic language

There are certain words that have more impact than others and can elicit certain behaviour. Words are evocative and incredibly powerful. They are so effective, either negatively or positively, they do work like magic and that's why we S-P-E-L-L them! The way they are said and how they are used in a sentence can encourage the behaviour or response you want or, indeed, have the opposite effect. One of the most common complaints I hear is "My kids don't listen to me" and "They never do as I say" (of course *never* isn't true! They do sometimes). Words like never, always, everyone and nobody are what we call universal quantifiers and are not true. They are exaggerations, not accurate. One reason children don't do as we ask, or seem not to listen, is because we're not telling them what we want, they may be listening and only hearing what you *don't* want!

Ditch your "don'ts"

You probably spend a lot of your time telling your children don't do this or don't do that, telling them what you don't want them to do, instead of asking them to do what you do want them to do. How many times do you hear yourself saying to younger children, "Don't run", "Don't jump on the furniture" and "Don't touch that", or to teenagers "Don't be late", "Don't leave your room a mess", "Don't lose your keys" and "Don't get drunk"? (If, of course, you know they might do!)

Reword what you say and ask them to do what you would like them to do. I'm not saying they always will, though the unconscious mind will be getting a clearer picture.

Let's reword the above. Change:

- "Don't run" to "Walk"
- "Don't jump on the furniture" to "Keep your feet on the floor" or "Please sit on the furniture"
- "Don't touch that" to "Leave that alone".

With older children instead of

- "Don't be late", "Be home on time"
- "Don't leave your room a mess", "Keep your room tidy"
- "Don't lose your keys", "Remember to keep your keys safe"
- "Don't get drunk", "Stay sober".

We bring their attention to and focus on negative stuff. Your unconscious mind can't directly process negatives. So, if I say to you "Don't think of an elephant", you have to think about an elephant (the thing you don't want to think about), before you can even attempt not to think about it! That being the case imagine what we're doing to our children. Even if you said "I didn't think of an elephant I thought of a giraffe", your mind had to think of an elephant to know that's not what you were to think of! It would be a two-step process because your mind cannot process a negative directly. Our mind immediately pictures things, we see them. If I ask you what your front door is like, you immediately find a picture of it, you see it in your mind. To finish on, don't think about a red double decker bus, or a computer!

Common mistakes parents make

Are to think that:

- Your children are mind readers. A lot of the time they don't know what you want, because you haven't told them!
- They look at the world the same way you do. Even if you want them to, it's good to remember they are wired differently. They are not a clone of you.
- Their priorities and values are the same as yours. Their priorities and values are the result of all the

influences on them, not just yours, and are relevant to their age and interests.
- Using the word don't will stop them doing what you don't want them to do. In fact, it actually highlights something they may not even have thought of.

Sit on your "buts"

Another word we use often is "but", it's a word that when we want to make an impact, stay positive and effective, is best avoided. But is a negation that takes away anything positive said before it!

Think about what happens when you hear someone say "but". You know something not so good is coming, don't you? For example, has anyone ever thanked you for something and then said, "but"? Remember how it feels. Your heart sinks, doesn't it? Now, think about when you've used it with your children. "Yes, that's a lovely picture, but we need to tidy up now", "Thanks for doing the washing up, but you could have cleaned the sides while you were at it" or "Yes, you have made your bed, but all your washing's on the floor."

The benefits of sitting on your buts
- Your child will hear that they're getting some things right, that you're pleased (with no down side!).
- Over time they will start to be more willing to listen to you.
- When they start to feel less criticized, they will tell you more about what they think. They'll open up to you more.

- Their confidence will start to improve and they'll be happier.
- They will become more communicative in every area of their lives.

How to reduce your buts

- Be aware of how often you say the word "but" and make a conscious decision to eliminate it.
- Be aware of how often other people use it and point it out to them in a supportive way.
- Replace "but" with "and", a positive building word. Use it with enthusiasm, and it turns criticism into feedback.
- Learn to use a feedback sandwich. Start with something positive; use "and" instead of "but" and then say what you want to change or improve; finish on an overall positive comment. If your teenager has made tea and made a mess in the kitchen, instead of saying: "Thanks for making tea but you've made a right mess", say "Thanks for making the tea and I'd really appreciate you tidying up as well please, it was really thoughtful and helpful of you to make tea tonight."

Say when

Say "when" instead of "if". "When" implies something will happen, it's just a matter of time. If allows more choice.

It's because

Get familiar with the magic word "because". It encourages compliance. It gives validity to what's said after it. After "because" we expect a reason, an explanation, a truth because that's what we usually get. As long as it's not just "Because I said so." You can have fun using "because": if you're in a supermarket queue and only have a few things in your basket, ask the person in front of you if they mind if you go before them. Say something like "You don't mind if I go before you, do you?" (they very well may already be saying go ahead) then you can qualify the request with "because I've put the wrong shoes on this morning and…" or "because I didn't have my porridge this morning and…" people are often not listening once you've made the request and started to tell them why!

Stop trying

Remember the words of the great philosopher Yoda "Do or do not, there is no try." Avoid saying "Try to…" simply say "do": encourage children to "do their best", that's all they can do, no need for the "try" first. It almost sets them up for failure, or gives them the option. Even when encouraging babies or children to eat something new, we can eliminate the "Just try some"; "Just have some" is a better directive… they either will or they won't.

When my youngest had finished his science exam one day and his father picked him up, he asked how it had gone. Eden said he didn't think it had gone too well. His dad said "Never mind, as long as you tried your best." Eden (remember he has me for a mother) said "I didn't try. I did my best." That's my boy!

First this... then

Two words that work well in a sentence when you want something doing and your child is doing or wants to do something else are "First… Then…", short and sweet, clear and concise. No need to add any more, just keep repeating it. The second part, the "then" works when it's something the child wants or something that you know is an incentive and will motivate them. It's also a case of less is more, the less we say the more effective it is. You can use it often enough for it to become a pattern they get to know, overusing it will cause it to lose its potency. You could also use the "When you have… Then…" Remember we want to encourage the "when" rather than an "if".

Feedback sandwich

This is often used for delivering criticism or feedback, framing it so it's in a positive way and is more likely to be taken on board.

When Eden was younger I used to have an issue with him leaving lots of stuff in his trouser pockets and causing broken washing machines because he would forget to empty them. It changed when I changed the way I dealt with it and what I said to him.

I had to find something positive about this situation first (rose coloured specs) so I would say, (making sure he was listening, getting eye contact), "Eden, I am really glad that you bring your rubbish home" (though that was a bit of a contentious issue, as to him it was "treasure"). I got rid of the "don't" that I would have started with, then said "*and* (this is where I would have said *but* in the past) what would be really helpful is *when* (not if) you empty them before they go in the washing machine *because* (valid reason going to be given) it's really helpful when you do that and I know (mind read/assumption) that you like helping me, don't you?"(tag question). This last question, "Don't you?", tagged on the end is to elicit agreement, accompanied with the body language of nodding my head to encourage him to nod and agree too (see Part 4 Chapter 6, Use tag questions).

> *Becoming aware of your negative language and changing it is like weeding a garden. When you take time to get rid of the weeds, the flowers have room to flourish and grow.*

Say something positive first, then give instruction or request (not criticism) and end on a positive.

When we stop focusing on negatives, they become less. We truly only bring into our lives what we focus on. Focus on what your child is doing right, is good at, has achieved, accomplished, there is always so much, be grateful for that. What we put our focus on grows, have you noticed that? I know once I'd got my Qashqai car, that I thought was fairly unusual, every other car I saw seemed to be one!

We may be adult and intelligent and think we know what we're saying and why – we don't! When we think, we are using the conscious part of our mind, which is only 5–10%. So much is coming from our unconscious programming and the language we use means something different to the unconscious mind, which is the bigger part. Let's look at the directives of the unconscious mind to understand this better.

The importance of the unconscious mind

We have already established that there are varying levels of consciousness and that a lot of our behaviour comes from programmes and wiring at the unconscious level, so it's important to understand what the unconscious mind is responsible for.

1. **Stores our memories** Our unconscious mind stores all of our memories.
2. **Organizes our memories** Using date, process of events, what was said, who was there, etc.
3. **Makes associations and learns quickly** Links similar things and experiences, so if you've perhaps tried a foreign food and not liked it, you may then decide you don't like foreign food. This ability helps us access information rapidly, though it's not always helpful. It generalizes.
4. **It is the domain of the emotions** While emotions may be experienced consciously, they are generated by, maintained by and are the responsibility of the unconscious mind.
5. **Represses memories with unresolved negative emotion** This is often because the person is not emotionally equipped to cope with the memory and the unconscious mind does this to protect the conscious mind.
6. **Presents repressed memories for resolution** The unconscious mind will present the repressed memory so that the unresolved negative emotion can be rectified, when the conscious mind is ready.
7. **Has a blueprint of and runs the body** Breathing, blinking, digestion of food, these are all processes that the body does without requiring guidance from us. The unconscious mind holds the blueprint of how the body should be and responds.
8. **Preserves the body** The unconscious mind maintains the integrity of the body and preserves it, this is its highest intention. It heals infection and damage and warns us of danger. In the event of crossing a road and a vehicle comes around a corner, it is most likely your unconscious mind that will rapidly advise you of the imminent danger

and create an instant response, e.g. stepping back onto the curb.

9. **Is our moral centre** Every person has their own moral code, generally based on their beliefs, their values and what they have been taught and accept.

10. **Enjoys taking direction and following orders** Our unconscious mind is like having an obedient child available. It wants to have clear direction from the conscious mind and will follow the instruction of the conscious mind. For successful outcomes the directions must be clear, consistent and focused. So make them positive ones. Maintain good rapport with the unconscious mind as it is diligently following orders.

11. **Controls and maintains all perceptions** We are bombarded with millions of pieces of information per second and expect instant understanding. For this purpose the unconscious mind must filter and manage this information so that we can respond instantly.

12. **Generates, stores, distributes and transmits energy throughout our body** The unconscious mind is responsible for managing and distributing our energy throughout our body. It can be requested to create energy for varying purposes, such as for healing.

13. **Responds with instinct and habit** Some behaviours are part of our genetic make-up, such as our fear responses of fight, flight or freeze. Others we can train ourselves in. The unconscious mind both generates and preserves our habits and instincts, both negative and positive.

14. **Requires repetition to instil new behaviours and therefore habits** All habits are instilled over time by

repetitive behaviour so it follows that change requires repetition in behaviours to create the new habit.

15. **Programmed to continually seek more** Our unconscious mind is always seeking more – new things, new achievements, more knowledge – and constantly asking "what's next?"

16. **Operates on the principle of minimum effort** Likes to take the "road of least resistance". It needs to conserve energy. For this purpose specific instruction and request is required.

17. **Functions at its best as a whole integrated unit** Our unconscious mind operates better with the fewer parts we have because more parts mean more internal conflict. In this reference "parts" may be goals, ideas, beliefs, some of which may conflict with each other. The unconscious mind works best as a whole unit and to ensure this the fewer parts, the better.

18. **Utilizes symbols** The unconscious mind creates, uses and responds to symbols. Much of the messaging it provides to us is symbolic. Think about the symbols the unconscious mind sends, they will have significance.

19. **Takes everything personally** Based upon the work completed by Carl Jung (Swiss psychologist and psychoanalyst, 1875–1961) what we like about another person are the aspects we like about ourselves. What we dislike about another person is reflecting what we dislike about ourselves. See and think the best of yourself and your unconscious mind will support that, see the opposite and it will respond accordingly.

20. **Does not process negatives directly** As we've already established. Remember do *not* think of an elephant, or a computer, or a tree. I'm sure you did, at least temporarily, before you pictured something

else. In order not to see something, we have to see what we do not want to see first!

Unconscious programming

Research states that only 5–10% of what we do is run by our conscious mind and 90–95% is run by our unconscious mind. (I don't know how they conducted their research!) I do know that so much of what we do is at the unconscious level. We don't consciously think to breathe, flow blood round our bodies, work out which muscles we need to use to write, hold a pen, a cup, walk, sit down, stand up. It all just happens, it's run by something, and this, as it's out of our conscious awareness, is called the unconscious or subconscious level. The 90–95% that is the unconscious mind is where thoughts and beliefs and patterns are stored, filed away as programmes we run without knowing. The unconscious mind is the part of you that is still child-like, takes everything literally and personally and knows the truth, so knows when we are lying.

Sigmund Freud (Austrian neurologist, 1856–1939) came up with the analogy of the mind as an iceberg and the bit sticking out of the water is all we used for doing things consciously, like making a decision and getting a drink of water, or picking up a pen. Though that bit is done consiously, the how we do it is all automatically programmed from a previous time, the actions to achieve the result, I mean.

These programmes come from childhood, where we record something we've seen, or heard, or something that's happened to us. Unfortunately a lot of the time what we actually do is record what that meant to us, what we thought it signified. We put meaning on it that isn't necessarily true. If, for instance, a parent says something to a child in anger on one particular occasion or the child is shouted at for something, the child will put a meaning on that, possibly, I'm not good enough, or I can't do anything right! While this isn't true, unfortunately human nature being what is is, we tend to remember and focus on that negative experience even though there will be many other positive ones. People attribute meaning to things that are said, situations and events and they are not going to have the same meaning for everyone.

One time (after we were divorced) my boys' dad was at our house and Hal, my middle son, was making us a hot drink. His dad was going on about what Hal 'should' be doing what he needed to do, find a college course and stick to it or a job and stay there longer than a few months. Hal had listened for long enough and finally flung the spoon he'd been using down the worktop and said "Well, I'm not going to be able to, am I? I'm Mr 30%", and left the kitchen to go upstairs to his room! His dad looked at me and said "What was all that about?" What all that was about was the fact that a long time ago, when Hal was at school and wasn't doing too well with school work, getting comments from teachers like "Could do better", "Needs to put more effort in", "Has to apply himself more", his father had been having a go at him for his behaviour and said "Whatever you do, Hal, you don't give it your all do you? You're Mr 30%." Ouch, it stuck!

I reminded his dad what he'd said and he couldn't even remember it. He obviously hadn't really meant it. It hadn't stuck in his memory. It certainly had in Hal's though.

It's always important to be aware of what we say and call our children. It can often stick. The old adage "Sticks and stones may break my bones but words will never hurt me" isn't quite true. Something that is said, either in jest or without thinking, can do a lot of damage.

Hal had chosen to believe what his dad had said and taken it to heart (and definitely to his unconscious mind), he was running that belief whether he was aware of it or not. He was fulfilling it, not sticking with college courses or jobs and thus proving his belief right. We do like to be right, don't we? It became a self-fulfilling prophecy. Hal had taken on board what was said to him and played it over in his mind, his thoughts, and that became a reality. I mentioned earlier how labels stick and even when we think children are not listening they often are. If we decide our children are anxious, nervous, shy, timid or whatever we may say to describe them, they hear it, take it on board and start to believe it. Be careful what you let your children hear you say, especially about them. I've heard parents say "He's a nightmare", or in earshot of their children "They're driving me mad, I'm sick of them". Not helpful for them to hear.

The unconscious mind knows the truth and isn't happy with lies (though repeat something often enough and you will see it, e.g. "I've got a terrible memory", "I'm not good at maths", etc.) Your unconscious mind, the universe, is always listening, in as much as the vibration of that goes out and comes back, to prove you right. It's like your personal genie, "Your wish is my command." Be careful what you wish for and say.

One of the directives and abilities of the unconscious mind is to know the truth and be honest, so it doesn't like it when we say we can't (when we mean we don't want to or aren't going to). This is often what happens when we are asked to do something we would rather not do, we automatically say "I can't", making up an excuse. Even when we say "I can't because I'm doing x or going to x", this still isn't a can't, it's an "I've already got plans that I am not going to change".

Even though we are adult and intelligent, at some level our unconscious mind knows it isn't true. This applies to our children, even more so when they are younger and still very much connected to their unconscious mind, haven't learnt too much yet and aren't programmed. We tell them they can't and they know they can!

Another great way to connect and communicate positively is to understand learning styles.

Know your child's learning style

We all have different learning styles, things that we are naturally good at because our brain is wired that way, and when we understand this it makes sense of why some children excel in one area and struggle in another. Often if a child seems bored, distracted or is struggling to learn something, it can be the teaching method that isn't helping.

The main learning styles are visual, auditory and kinaesthetic (often read/write is also included) and usually we have a mix of them with one preferred style of learning. This explains why some children aren't too good at certain things. A child who is kinaesthetic (Eden is) likes to be physical, use their hands, do, touch and feel. They are often good at sport or doing activities such as cooking, making models, building things, fixing things, and not so good at the more academic subjects that require reading and writing, as these involve visual and auditory learning styles. It can explain why some children really struggle with spelling and concentrating on reading; they get bored, they're not playing to their strength when they are wired to be doing and moving. This lack of attention in that area or subject and inability to learn is often why they misbehave or are distracted, and can then be labelled with Attention Deficit Disorder. When we know their style, we can use the language that most appeals to them and will have most impact. You can hear it in their language, in anyone's language, e.g. in the following phone calls I made. One to my bank, the lady I spoke to said she would look into it and see what had happened. After a while she said, she'd got the picture and told me it looked like... then proceeded to tell me what had happened. Her language was visual. I had another phone call with an insurance company and the gentleman there told me he would get to the bottom of it, after a while he said he thought he had got to grips with what had happened, that he had a handle on it and he had concrete evidence of what had happened. Very kinaesthetic language. All of us do use all kinds, of course, though we tend to have a preference.

My youngest son, Eden, struggled with reading and writing. In fact when he went to mainstream secondary school, after being at a special needs school, he could barely read or write three letter words. It was after I had discovered the spelling strategy while studying NLP that things changed. I was able to find out Eden's learning style (he was kinaesthetic) and put in place a strategy for him to access visual recall to help him learn spellings. See my YouTube video where I discuss this in more detail (https://www.youtube.com/watch?v=yHar9HVgdHc). This strategy can be found in The User's Manual for the Brain by Bob Bodenhamer and L. Michael Hall.[4]

---

[4] Bob G. Bodenhamer, and L. Michael Hall The User's Manual for the Brain Vol 1: The Complete Manual for Neuro-Linguistic Programming Practitioner Certification (Crown House Publishing revised edition 2000).

Our model of the world

We each have our own view of the world. In NLP we call it our "Model of the world". We each see it differently. We know this is true, think about how differently people view the same thing. A road traffic accident for example, or some crime. Each eye witness statement will differ, some greatly, from others, even though they are describing the same incident! How we process information is different, how and what we retain is different and the language we use is different.

A car accident, for instance, might be described by one person as "The cars bumped into each other", another might say "hit" and another might use the word "crashed". Even the difference in one word paints a different picture for the listener. When describing the height of a person involved, one person may consider them "not very tall", another "quite tall", it's all perspective. The words used can also have an effect on the memory of someone when they recall an incident. Often lawyers in court use language and word their questions in such a way as to influence the memory of the person being questioned. These are known as leading questions and this happens in life, not just in court rooms.[5]

Albert Mehrabian (a psychologist born 1939 to an Armenian family living in Iran) when talking about face to face communication, either one to one or one to many, claimed research showed only 7% of communication was relayed or received by words, 38% by tone and 55%

---

[5] See Loftus and Palmer Study for more information, www. simplypsychology.org/loftus-palmer.html [accessed April 2020].

by body language.[6] Considering this, it's not surprising a lot of miscommunication, misinterpretation and misunderstanding happens with the written word, in the absence of tone and body language. Think about text messages, emails, Facebook posts etc. The meaning comes from the way the person is reading it, interprets it, not necessarily the way the person writing it meant. Without tone and body language a lot of information is not present.

Body language

We are communicating very well when we use our bodies, either in subtle, small gestures or large actions, i.e. behaviour. A person who raises their eyebrows after a comment is made either by themselves or somebody else is communicating something, in much the same way as a person taking part in a riot and throwing things is communicating something. Body language plays a big part in communication. This is worth remembering when we think of what happens with our children. Toddlers don't have the words and yet we know how they are feeling by their behaviour, their body language. Teenagers prove this too. When they are stomping around the house banging doors and, when asked "What's the matter?", reply "Nothing" in a tone that suggests something clearly is. I had plenty of proof of this when I had teenagers at home. If one of them came home in a bad mood, banging about the place, school bag thrown down the hall, slamming doors and walking straight past me, I'd ask "What's wrong?" I'd often get the reply "Nothing! I'm FINE!" said in a tone that definitely indicated they were anything but!

---

[6] Albert Mehrabian *Silent Messages: Communication of Emotions and Attitudes* (Wadsworth Publishing Company 1972).

We obviously relay messages and meaning with our body, we're used to the term body language. We can read it. Remember, however, we might not always be right about what a person's body language is saying. It's easy to label it, though the labels aren't always right. Folded arms are often described as defensive. They aren't always, someone might be cold or just comfortable folding their arms. Think about this when we're putting meaning on our children's body language. A toddler who looks angry may be, though they also might be confused or frustrated and not know how to handle or express themselves, or even label what's happening for them. We react to what we think is happening. With teenagers, what we think it means or looks like might not be how it is. Teenagers can often adopt a certain way of being, looking or behaving that has more to do with keeping up appearances, with acting in the same way as other teenagers.

Kinetic parenting

Kinetic parenting is the way we parent. The definition of kinetic being "relating to or resulting from motion" or movement of something, in this case, us![7] Our parenting is done through how we Be, Do and Say things with or to our children, or to others that they observe, whether we think it is or not. All communication has energy, every breath you take, every move you make, every word you say… they'll be watching you (can't help but hear The Police song!). Children are recording devices, their minds, especially their unconscious minds, absorb and store information that isn't always accurate (as it will have the meaning they have put on it): not always helpful.

---

[7] www.lexico.com/definition/kinetic [accessed April 2020].

Behaviour, actions and the bigger, noticeable movements of the body are kinetic and other smaller movements such as gestures, eye movements and ideomotor responses are kinesic communication. Ideomotor responses are unconscious, involuntary movements caused by some stimuli, these as well as other behaviours we exhibit are often due to our wiring at the unconscious level. We are, whether we like it or not, programmed, wired to think, believe and run programmes that have been installed without our knowing it. They are very often unhelpful, limiting beliefs we carry and unfortunately pass on to our children. The energy we emit carries information absorbed by our children and can then be adopted by our children, just as generational patterns are passed on too. We are communicating to our children, and everyone else for that matter, whether we are speaking or not. Our heart is the strongest electromagnetic generator. The energetic field from the heart is 60 times greater than that of the brain. The Institute of HeartMath has carried out extensive research in this field.[8] When we think and feel positive intention, feel love from our heart, that is the first point of positive communication.

This energetic movement and motion means we are constantly communicating with our energy and what's held in it, this is natural kinetic communication, it's happening all the time. Our energy is reflected in our emotions, thoughts and beliefs. The energy of us, of human beings, any living thing (or non-living for that matter) is always moving, it's never absolutely still, energy is always moving, it moves at different frequencies. We act according to our beliefs and thoughts. If a person jumps a mile when

---

[8] Rollin McCraty, The Energetic Heart: Bioelectromagnetic Interactions Within and Between People (E-booklet published by HeartMath Institute 2002).

someone has thrown a piece of rope into the room where they are because they think it's a snake, even for an instant, and they are terrified of snakes, they react accordingly. What is your behaviour saying to your children, what are you teaching them?

You know how different emotions feel in the body. A great, positive emotion, like happiness, excitement, love, joy, peace, all feel very different to low frequency, negative emotions, like fear, guilt, shame, anger, etc. Each emotion has its own vibration or frequency. There is an emotional scale we all experience and have our own set points. In his book *Power vs. Force* Dr David Hawkins calls it the Levels of Consciousness.[9] In Yvette Taylor's *The Ultimate Self-Help Book* she also provides an emotional scale.[10]

We know we pass on so much learnt behaviour, e.g. if you are afraid of, have a phobia of, or just don't like something, spiders, bees, cotton wool (yes I have come across that), then our children often have the same fear or dislike. We've taught them through our reactions, behaviours, what we've said and from the energy we have transmitted, through that oh so effective electromagnetic field.

---

[9] David R. Hawkins *Power vs. Force: The Hidden Determinants of Human Behaviour* (Hay House 2002).
[10] Yvette Taylor *The Ultimate Self-Help Book: How to be Happy, Confident and Stress Free* (Make Your Mark Global Publishing 2018).

Part 4

Brain and child development

Chapter 5

How the brain functions and child develops

Understanding our "happy" chemicals

The brain produces chemicals that are responsible for feel good factors and are necessary for a healthy brain and good life balance. Dopamine, serotonin, endorphins and oxytocin are types of chemicals known as a neurotransmitters. They are different types of neurotransmitters and there are many different types of each. The brain is made up of long cells known as neurons, which pass signals, in the form of electrical currents, from one to the next. In between each neuron is an extremely small gap called a synapse. To send the signal from one neuron to the next, the signal needs to jump this gap. In order to do this, the neuron sending the signal releases neurotransmitters into the synapse, which float across and bind to the receiving neuron. This then affects the activity of the receiving neuron either by increasing or decreasing its electrical activity, which has an effect on how we feel.

Dopamine

Dopamine motivates us to take action toward goals, desires and needs, and gives a surge of reinforcing pleasure when achieving them. Procrastination, self-doubt and lack of enthusiasm are linked with having low levels of dopamine. We need change and challenge in our lives so that we can feel a sense of achievement in accomplishing something new. Our need for dopamine keeps us driven, ambitious and looking for new and different experiences. Sometimes making that change or achieving that goal can be overwhelming, so break big goals down into little pieces. We can create a series of little finish lines, with dopamine being released each time we reach one, and it's crucial to celebrate them.

Serotonin

Serotonin flows when you feel significant or important, so when we've achieved and succeeded and are recognized for it, acknowledged and given respect, no wonder we feel good, there's a lot of dopamine and serotonin being released. Loneliness and depression appear when serotonin is absent. Unhealthy, attention-seeking behaviour can also be a cry for what serotonin brings, so remember this with your child if they're behaving badly. Bad behaviour is often simply a cry for attention and it's not for no good reason, the body is looking for a way to get its serotonin fix. This need could be part of the explanation of why our teenagers join gangs, get in with the wrong crowd or involved in criminal activity.

Endorphins

Endorphins are released in response to pain. We often hear about or may have experienced the surging second wind and euphoric runner's high during or after a vigorous run. This is a result of endorphins. Similar to morphine, they act as an analgesic and sedative, helping us push through the pain barrier. Along with regular exercise, laughter is one of the easiest ways to induce endorphin release. Finding several things to laugh at during the day is a great way to keep the doctor away. The smell of vanilla and lavender has been linked with the production of endorphins. Studies have shown that dark chocolate and spicy foods can also lead the brain to release endorphins.

I used to use lavender oil when Eden was a toddler, in a diffuser, a drop or two in fractionated coconut oil on his pillow or for a massage. He loved it. In fact, on one occasion when I had company and hadn't put any on his pillow, he asked if he could have some of that stuff that made him feel all "woozy"… I'm not sure what people thought I was giving him!

Oxytocin

Oxytocin creates intimacy, trust and builds healthy relationships. It's produced by mothers during childbirth and breastfeeding. The cultivation of oxytocin is essential for creating strong bonds and improved social interactions. It can be cultivated and encouraged by touch. Often referred to as the cuddle hormone, a simple way to keep oxytocin flowing is to give someone a hug.

Dr Paul Zak (American neuroeconomist known as Dr Love, born 1962) explains that inter-personal touch not only raises oxytocin, but reduces cardiovascular stress and improves the immune system; rather than just a hand shake, go in for the hug. Dr Zak recommends eight hugs each day.[1] He has now found evidence that a hug lasting 20 seconds is most beneficial.

---

[1] Dr Paul Zak *The Moral Molecule: The Source of Love and Prosperity* (Dutton 2012). See also his TED Talk, 'Trust, morality – and oxytocin?' at www.ted.com/talks/paul_zak_trust_morality_and_oxytocin [accessed April 2020].

Virginia Satir (American author, social worker and psychotherapist, 1916–1988), known especially for her approach to family therapy and her work with family reconstruction, said that we need hugs every day: four for survival, eight for maintenance and twelve to grow.

Touch is important, feeling connected is important and it's easy to see why Facebook and social media have become so important in some people's lives. They get their connection and are in *touch* with people. That's a good thing and it is satisfying a basic human need. It's important to keep that connection positive though. So use it for good. Share and like good, uplifting, positive posts and avoid any negativity. If you post on there, you'll know it's a good feeling when people like it. We all like to be liked.

When someone receives a gift their oxytocin levels can rise. You can strengthen your relationship and help your children by touch, hugs or gifts; they don't have to be expensive, bought gifts either. Take time to make something just that little bit more special for them. I often used to do it when making breakfast, I'd cut the toast into heart shapes and put it on a tray with a little post it note saying "I love you" or "You make my heart glow", anything that was positive.

Remember all the above applies to you and your children, their brain make-up is the same as yours.

The importance of the early years

The early years of a child's life are very important for their health and development. They are affected by so many factors. The natural development of the brain and environmental factors play a huge part. My very good friend Deborah McNelis (founder of Brain Insights) is a brain development specialist and has this to say:

A child's brain is far from being fully developed at birth. It continues to develop until about the age of 25, with the early months and years being extremely critical to well-being in life.

The term "brain development" refers to much more than influencing how smart a child is. It is the actual physical growth that takes place in the brain. The very influential early months and years of a child's life are the time for the most rapid brain growth which influences not only learning, but relationships, self-esteem, overall physical development and health as well.

Resent research findings estimate that a young child may be developing brain connections at a rate of 1 million per second. The wonderful news is, informed and caring adults can have a very positive influence on this development.

The brain is experience dependent. The growing brain is influenced of course by genetics, but additionally the types of experiences a child has makes an incredible difference. In the absence of experiences, a brain will not grow. It relies on experiences to make the necessary connections between the billions of brain cells a baby has at birth. The experiences a child has in the first few years determine the way in which brain pathways are formed and reinforced to create a basic foundation for functioning in life.

Nutrition, sleep, regular routines, physical activity, direct interactive language, play, feelings of safety and predictable nurturing experiences with caring adults positively influence the way brain pathways are created and also determine the brain areas that are strengthened most. These optimal experiences directly contribute to a brain that is healthy, ready to get along with others, and is eager for continuous learning.

However, constant exposure to stress, limited stimulation, poor nutrition, chaos and lack of consistent nurturing relationships all create a brain that is "wired" in a way that can potentially lead to emotional, learning and health problems. The growing brain of a child will adapt to the type of environment and experiences that a child is exposed to most frequently.

A developing brain will simply adapt to a negative environment or repeated experiences just as easily as it will adapt to a positive environment and experiences. This adaptation happens through a "use it or lose it" process. The connections that are frequently used due to repetition are retained and become stronger. Other connections that are not used often will be pruned or eliminated.

So, of course, it is most advantageous to regularly provide the optimal experiences. If the essential elements of meeting physical and security needs, providing nurturing interactions and an abundance of play are the most frequent experiences, the brain will develop in ways that will contribute to a child who develops the highest functioning brain areas. When fully developed these higher function brain areas support important abilities such as self-regulation, empathy, critical thinking, controlling impulses, imagination, anticipating consequences, thinking in the abstract and planning.

Consistently responsive, predictable and nurturing relationships are the essential place to begin optimal brain development. When children benefit from the adults in their lives fully understanding and then providing what they need most, this allows the uniquely beautiful essence within a child to shine brilliantly.

Deborah McNelis M.Ed, Brain Insights Founder and Creator of Neuro-Nurturing

As Deborah says, the first years are critical to a child's development. It's said that the first three years see the most rapid rate of brain connections being made based on experiences. There is also a school of thought that talks about the first 1,000 critical days (conception to age two) being most important and it is also said that it's the first five years that critically impact the growth and development of the brain.[2] Here's an idea of what to expect.

Child development from birth to age three

One to six months

At the very beginning, your baby is primarily focused on immediate needs such as food, love and attention. In these first few months, if your baby feels loved and secure and is having their needs met, they are happy and well and blissfully unaware of very much else. Much of their time and energy will be spent watching you, strengthening muscles, gaining control over reflexes and coordinating visual abilities with hand movements. They are dependent on you for their every need. They think that you and they are one and the same. They become attached to the caregiver (usually the mother) to form a secure attachment. They don't like to be separated and one of the first ways that babies express this is by crying to attract your attention. Your baby is growing increasingly aware that their behaviour affects others, mainly you, and they soon learn the connection between their crying, i.e. their behaviour and your behaviour. If every time your baby cries you pick them up, they will make this connection

---

[2] G.C. Davenport *An Introduction to Child Development* (Collins Educational second edition 1997) and Kathleen McCartney and Deborah Phillips (eds) *Blackwell Handbook of Early Childhood Development* (Blackwell Publishing 2006).

and expect this response every time and then be distressed when or if it doesn't work. This is how the brain gets wired and they begin to understand that if I do A then I get B. This behaviour is known as operant conditioning.

Babies crying is one way of communicating and it's up to the parent/carer to find out the reason. Their first cry is a stress response to being born into this world. It's a big change. Be aware of not making too many changes. The earlier a routine is established the better. Be aware of how different it is for them at different times of the day and how they respond so you can start to realize what it is that's upsetting or unsettling them. Think how different their day is to their evening. Perhaps in the day it's very quiet, only one parent home, no other children, no TV etc., then in evening or later in the day siblings come home, father comes home from work, more people, more noise. More stimulation. Let this become the time for calm and comfort, find a quiet place, no extra noise, just soothing music perhaps, and let them spend time with you, encouraging sleep and rest, if this is at all possible.

We know human touch and contact is very important and baby massage is an excellent way of being really connected with your child. It helps stimulate blood flow, keeps muscles flexible, and it's an enjoyable and beneficial experience. Peter Walker, Physical Therapist and leading expert on baby massage, has this to say: "Following the birth it is touch that helps to continue this growing connection and the language of mutual learning about one another."

Crying in very young babies is always for a reason, they are signalling something and you might not always know what that is. Check everything you can think of, are they hungry, uncomfortable, need changing or moving into a different position? When you have checked everything you can leave them alone as long as it's safe. Especially if you are stressed, or anxious, picking up baby in that state won't help solve the problem or calm the baby, energetic exchange in this state will probably make it worse.

Do your best to have a backup plan for a break, a trusted friend, relative, call in the cavalry when you need it. Pushing yourself will only lead to you reaching a point where you can't cope, so tell someone if you're not coping or you need help. If you don't get it, it can lead to feelings of anger and resentment, which can lead to harming the baby and/or depression in the parent. Talk about it, reach out at any stage if you're finding your children challenging.

By six months you may notice that your baby starts to want to communicate, interact more and will respond readily to your voice, smiles and chatter.

Six to 12 months

Now your baby has realized they are a separate being. Though they still may become distressed and start crying when you leave them, even for a short while. At this age they are still too young to understand that you will be back. If you do leave your baby to be cared for by someone else, it helps to say goodbye and go while they are watching. Explain that you will return soon even if you are not sure that they understand you, it is reassuring and can be reflected in your voice, tone and facial expression. Sneaking out while their back is turned won't help, it may just make them anxious when they realize you're not there and more afraid that you aren't coming back.

They gain needed trust through your predictable responsiveness to become more secure, more sociable and confident with others.

If you leave your little one with a new person or your separations are less regular, it may take them longer to get used to being parted. They will in time get to know that you always come back. Reassure your baby by giving them something that they often see you using or wearing, like a soft scarf. The chances are that it will smell of you, which will give added comfort.

Twelve to 24 months

Your baby will start to become their own person, when a secure attachment is established, growing in confidence and making progress in differentiating themself from you and from the world around them.

They may still get upset when you leave them at nursery or with a babysitter, though they will recover much quicker. I have witnessed it many times in nurseries, when a child is left and they can still see the parent who has dropped them off, they cry, but almost as soon as the parent is out of sight they stop! They are beginning to know they are safe and quite like being where they are, they are simply running a response mechanism that they have learned and it is programmed for them to run it.

Feeling secure and loved gives your baby the confidence they need to express likes, dislikes and opinions as they grow older. It may be exhausting for you when your toddler insists on wearing their spotty pyjamas for the tenth night in a row and only eating certain foods. Still, it's a good thing to remember to not make too much out of a certain behaviour and allow it where possible. This creates self-confidence and a sense of belonging and security and leads to a more independent child. Very often as parents we get hung up on the small stuff that doesn't really matter. It's us who have the worry and concerns and think we can't let them do whatever it is they want to and we can't let them get away with it, because it will cause problems later or we're not being a good parent. Truthfully, though, a lot of the time it doesn't matter, what a child wants to wear isn't all that important and it's good to realize that it's us, most of the time, that think we can't take them out looking like that! Yes we can. We'll all live and get over it.

Some parents may think they need to be insistent and a child needs to learn they can't always have their own way and have to learn to do as they are told, and while this is true to a certain extent, it's important to know at what age we can start to negotiate with them and there are ways of fostering compliance that work better than others. Being dictatorial and too authoritative doesn't work well and often backfires.

Most things our toddlers want to do, they very quickly outgrow and when we look back we realize it was no big deal really. We're the ones who make it so. When my youngest son was little he insisted on wearing a navy blue tee shirt all the time, under anything he wore, even pyjamas. I solved it by buying two so there was always one clean. He doesn't do this anymore, interestingly enough. I can't remember when he stopped wanting to, I just know he did!

Twenty-four to 36 months

Between the ages of two and three years old, your toddler will continue to grow more independent. This is where trouble can start. We confuse them. We want our children to grow up independent, confident and feeling comfortable and when they start to want to go off on their own, in supermarkets for example, we shout at them and call them back and want them to do as we say. They haven't done anything wrong, it's a testament to what you're doing right. Of course, we want to keep them safe and have them listen to us and respond, we don't want to frighten them, tell them off and send mix messages. It's okay for you to be on your own when I take you to nursery and you can wander around there exploring, not in a supermarket though. They haven't got the logic or the understanding yet of the difference, so be gentle with them.

Wanting things their own way is at the heart of many temper tantrums and being two years old is known as the terrible twos for a good reason. "I can do it myself" is probably one of the most common phrases parents hear from older toddlers, along with "No!"

This is an exciting time for toddlers. They are realizing that they are separate individuals from their parents and caregivers. This means that they are driven to assert themselves, to communicate their likes and dislikes and to act independently (as much as they can). Toddlers are also developing the language skills that help them express their ideas, wants and needs.

At the same time, toddlers do not understand logic and still have a hard time with waiting and self-control. They are aware of feelings they are experiencing, i.e. emotions, and often two-year-olds want what they want when they want it. This is why you may be hearing things like "no" and "me do it". They are starting to see or experience themselves as separate beings, separate from you.

Dealing with strong emotions

Now they are beginning to experience feelings like pride, shame, guilt and embarrassment for the first time.

Older toddlers are a lot like teenagers. Their feelings may swing wildly from moment to moment. They may be really happy when getting an ice cream and then despair when it drips on their hands. They really need your loving guidance to figure out how to cope with their emotions. Your child is struggling with this when:

- They have a meltdown when you can't understand their words.
- They say no when they mean yes (you are offering a favourite treat).
- They get so angry that they might throw a toy or their food.
- They cannot settle for a substitute – if the purple pyjamas are in the wash, they are inconsolable (even though you have offered the green ones, the polka dot ones, the ones with unicorns or dinosaurs on).
- They act out when frustrated – will give up or get angry when they can't figure out how to make a shape fit in a shape sorter, or how to make something work.

Your child is learning to manage strong feelings when they do the following instead of the above:

- Use words or actions to get your attention or ask for help.
- Talk to themself in a reassuring way when they are frustrated or frightened. For example, they might say to themself "Daddy will come back" after you drop them off at child care, or "I can build this again" after their block tower collapses.
- Re-enact a stressful event, like a doctor's visit, or taking the dog to the vet.
- Use words like "I'm mad" rather than throwing or hitting.

- Tell you the rules or show that they feel badly about breaking rules. For example, your child might say "no, not…" to themself as they do something off-limits, like opening the fridge. Or they might tell you at the park, "No walking in front of the swings."

Learning self-control

When you see challenging behaviour, it usually means that your child can't figure out how to express their feelings in an acceptable way or doesn't know how to get a need met. What helps your child learn is when your response shows a different, more constructive way to handle these feelings.

Learning to cope with strong feelings usually happens naturally as children develop better language skills in their third year and have more experience with peers, handling disappointment and following rules. What follow are some ideas for helping your toddler begin to learn this important skill.

Talk about feelings

Read books and notice aloud how the characters are feeling. The dog is really happy that he got a bone. I bet you're happy when you get something you like. Share your own feelings, "I just spilled my drink, I feel really frustrated and a bit annoyed! I'd like your help to wipe it up" and when they do say "It feels really good to have your help". When your child can label how they are feeling, it helps them begin to gain control over their emotions and communicate them to others. Though as mentioned earlier, when using EAM we don't always have to label emotions.

Young children need guidance when it comes to dealing with big feelings like anger, sadness and frustration, even excitement. So always validate them. When your child is really angry, acknowledge what they are experiencing: "You are really angry right now because I said no more television."

Then suggest that they jump up and down, hit the sofa cushions, rip paper, cuddle up in a cosy area for alone time, paint an angry picture or some other strategy that you feel is appropriate. Teach your child that there are many options for expressing their feelings in healthy, non-hurtful ways. Depending on the age of the child EAM is always an option.

Empathy and understanding

Let them know that you understand the choices they are being offered are not the ones they want: "We have to leave now to go to Sharon's. I know you'd rather stay home with me. You miss me and I miss you during the day. That's not a choice today. I am going to work. When we both get home we will finish the puzzle we started and have a lovely tea." Then distract and find a sentence you can add a tag question onto (see Part 4 Chapter 6, Use tag questions) and affirm with positive body language, e.g. "Let's get in the car now and you can put your seat belt on yourself, can't you?"

Visual aids for waiting

If your child has to wait until their soup has cooled down, show them the steam rising from the bowl. Tell them that when the steam goes away, you can test the soup on a spoon to see if it is cool enough. To help your child brush their teeth for two minutes each day, use an egg timer so they can watch the countdown. Need 10 minutes to do a chore? Set a kitchen timer so that your child can keep track. Let them know you know it's difficult for them to wait, acknowledge that.

Choices

Let them choose what to wear (two choices, three at most) and what to eat (within reason), what to play, who to play with. This gives them a feeling of control and supports growing confidence and a sense of competency.

Offering choices also helps head off the "not that one" game where you keep offering your child different things and they keep saying "Not that one, the other one!" Instead, try giving your child three choices and let them pick: "You can have an apple, a string cheese or a bagel for a snack. What sounds good to you?"

Sharing

Introduce games that require turn-taking, great for practising how to wait and share. Rolling a ball back and forth is an example. This game gives children the chance to wait and control their impulse to grab the ball. Another idea is playing "sharing music" where each of you chooses an instrument to play and set an egg timer for one minute. When the timer goes off, switch instruments and set the timer again.

Challenging behaviour

What might be considered challenging behaviour by one person might not be by another. Remember your child's learning style has a lot to do with their behaviour. A child who can't sit still when asked to, or doesn't listen well or retain what you've said could be a kinaesthetic learner (see Part 3 Chapter 4, Know your child's learning style). Some people can handle situations that others would find difficult and challenging without having a melt-down, losing their temper or feeling frustrated or embarrassed. It's more about the person dealing with the situation than it is the incident itself. We often hear the word misbehaviour or defiant behaviour. It's important to remember that even though you may consider it or call it that, most of the time, in that moment, it's the only "behaviour" the child or young person can exhibit. Of course there are behaviours that sometimes truly do seem to be simply destructive and defiant; still, it helps to remember that the behaviour has come from somewhere. There is a reason for it. It is driven by emotions or feelings and often because they cannot express what they are feeling, experiencing in any other way. Of course, there still have to be consequences, though it is a cry for help. They are not liking whatever is happening to them, or in their life. They haven't mastered their emotions yet and there are a lot of adults who haven't mastered that self-control yet either!

By the time children start school, defiance is part and parcel of their behavioural repertoire. It includes outright refusals to comply with requests, doing what you've asked them not to, breaking rules, arguing, blaming others. They are finding their place in the world and not knowing how else to express this yet, often resulting in outbursts of emotions expressing anger or frustration. This behaviour is similar to what's going on for our teenagers, too. This is normal and whilst not easy to deal with, if we are best prepared we can prevent what become the really difficult challenges later. As children get older their defiance can be more manipulative or at least more questioning, such as why do we have to have these stupid rules and what are often referred to as power struggles ensue. This is how they express their need to assert themselves and test their rightful place in the world, which is a necessary part of growing up and becoming independent. This behaviour often causes the adult dealing with it to feel threatened or not in control, their authority is being questioned. We need to be in a strong and confident position and have some strategies to be able to deal with this kind of behaviour. Once we are forewarned we can be forearmed.

Challenges we have when children and young people aren't behaving as we want them to are often labelled Oppositional Defiant Behaviour (ODB) or Oppositional Defiant Disorder (ODD), where children have disruptive and oppositional behaviour that is particularly directed towards authority figures, such as parents or teachers. If it gets to this, seek help, of course.

- **Strategies for managing aggression in young children.** Limits are part of loving. Remember when your child's feeling loved, cared for and valued it builds the foundation for their acceptance of the guidance you will provide as they grow. Children who feel loved want to please their parents most of the time and will respond to their guidance. Putting reasonable restrictions on your child's behaviour is part of loving them.
- **Identify what triggered the aggressive behaviour.** Ask yourself what might have happened that set them off. Perhaps they are overtired or not feeling well physically. Being rushed, abruptly handled, being denied something they want, even being unable to do something they have tried to do with a toy or physical activity often produces feelings of frustration and anger that result in aggressive behaviour. The end result they exhibit

may have been triggered by something seemingly unrelated.

- **Use your inside information.** Make use of what you know about your child's temperament, rhythms, preferences and sensitivities. For example, if you know that they are irritable or ill-humoured for the first hour of the day or get very out of sorts when tired or hungry, that's not a good time to change routine (if avoidable) and not a great time to expect much control or compliance from them.
- **Be clear with instruction.** Tell your child what you want them to do, focusing on what you do want, not on what you don't want. Make it clear, concise and avoid giving a long lecture. Your child will be aware of your displeasure from your tone of voice as well as from what you say.
- **Be clear about your disapproval.** It is important that you are clear about your disapproval. Avoid the long lectures and dire predictions of what might happen if… This is usually counterproductive. Telling a three-year-old child that they can't have any television for two weeks if they hit their baby brother may upset them, but it is unlikely to help them understand and develop their own self-control. It's more helpful to explain that you don't want them to hit him because it hurts. It helps any young child who has earned the disapproval of a parent be reminded that they are loved even when you don't like the behaviour. The child is not the behaviour.
- **Be a careful observer.** When your child is playing with other children, keep an eye on the situation without being intrusive. What begins as playful scuffling or run and chase or sharing toys can quickly turn into a battle between children and

they may need a referee. However, there are times when you can let young children work things out among themselves. Age makes a difference, of course.

- **Use redirection.** When your child is being aggressive in ways you don't like, stop the behaviour and give them something else to do. Either suggest or help start a new activity or guide them to a place where they can discharge aggressive feelings without doing harm to themself, to anyone or anything else. For example, a corner in which there is something to punch or throw can be utilized. You can say, for example, "If you feel like hitting, go and hit your pillow (or punching bag), not the dog or the table with a hammer!" This not only helps the child discharge some aggressive feelings, it also helps them understand that there can be a time and place provided for such actions. It's important to let them know that all emotions are allowed, they just need to be discharged appropriately. Rather than teach children it's wrong to get angry or upset about things, validate their emotions and help them deal with them.

- **Be a coach.** When you can, demonstrate how to handle a situation in which there is conflict between children. For instance, if your child is old enough, you can teach them a few words to use in order to avoid or settle a conflict. A two-year-old can be helped to hold on to a toy and say "no" or "mine" instead of always pushing or crying or hitting when another child tries to take a toy. Children need specific suggestions and demonstrations from adults in order to learn that there are effective ways to handle disagreements that are more acceptable than physical attack and retaliation.

- **Use language.** If your child has language skills, help them explain what they are angry about. If you are able to guess and they cannot say, do it for them, such as, "I guess you're mad because you can't go to play with Johnny. I know how you feel, but it's too late to go today" (or whatever the reason is). If they can express it and respond, ask the questions "Are you mad because...?" Accept their response and then offer an explanation or reason for whatever it is. Remember to empathize.

- **Avoid sending mixed messages.** If you say "Don't hit" (though I'm sure you're eliminating your don'ts) or "Be nice" while you are secretly enjoying your child's aggressive behaviour towards someone else, or find it amusing, they will be confused and such confusions tend to make it more difficult to develop self-control. They need consistency.

- **Avoid physical punishment.** Think about the very real disadvantages of physical punishment for your child. Children often arouse anger in adults when they provoke, tease, behave stubbornly or attack others. If you hit or physically punish your child, you are teaching it's okay to be physically aggressive towards others. You are the person they trust not to hurt them.

- **Be patient.** Your child's learning to live in reasonable harmony with others takes time. You'll have ups and downs, periods of despair when you think you'll never get through to your child or teach them. Times when you will wonder whether they will ever be civil or be too timid to cope in the world. Remain calm and present and keep the long-term view in mind, there is a positive momentum to development. This trajectory of your child's growth and development actually works in favour of acquiring the ability to channel and productively use aggressive energies that are a vital part of our make-up, needed to survive and thrive.

Parents sometimes tell me about their toddler who knows better than to hit or bite. They believe this is so because when they are scolded, they look ashamed and know they have done something wrong. Rather than understand what they have done, i.e. hurt someone or destroyed something, they know they have earned the disapproval of their parents. Conversely, when praised for being gentle with another, doing something good or being kind, they know and are pleased that they have the approval of parents for that behaviour at that moment, not necessarily making the connection. It will take time and many instances and reminders before they can make the connection and understand that not hitting or biting applies to many situations. Young children, particularly those under three or four, scarcely know their own strength. The differences between a kiss and a bite, between patting and hitting, between nudging and pushing someone down are not automatically understood and children need many reminders, such as "Let me show you how to pat the baby (or the family dog or Daddy's cheek)", "Patting feels nice. Hitting can hurt" or "Do it softly (or gently), like this."

How you show ways of dealing with anger and aggression are setting the example. If social exchanges in your family include much arguing or physical fighting in the presence or hearing of your children, then they'll pick that up.

We often call the confrontations we have with our children power struggles and they are natural, we are always going to have them, they're part of life, our children learning to stand on their own two feet, growing up, and they're necessary to have for them (and us) to know how to handle them, be assertive and be independent human beings.

Power struggles often occur in the teenage years so let's look at understanding them better. There are ways we can find cooperation instead of confrontation, can turn chaos into order and unrest into peace and calm.

Teenage challenges

Teenage years can be difficult and it helps to understand that their brain is going through lots of changes. The brain has an amazing capacity to keep developing, the plasticity of the brain means it can continue to develop indefinitely, affected by the environment it is living in and the experiences it encounters. The teenage brain is not fully developed and different bits of it develop at different times, accounting for what we may consider to be the odd, difficult and troublesome behaviour.[3] In comparison to a fully developed brain where all the bits have been joined up or connected theirs haven't yet! It's like having an entertainment consul or centre where we know we need all the bits, wires and connectors to be plugged in at the same time or it just doesn't work properly, our teens may have bits not plugged in yet or have loose connections.

Understanding that they can't help being clumsy and that they do need more sleep because of the changes their brain and body are going through, helps. The development of their brain is not something we can change. However, we can alter the way we behave towards them and thus prevent some challenging behaviour.

When we want our teenagers to listen to us, we have to find a way of communicating so that they hear what we're

---

[3] Bruce H. Lipton *The Biology of Belief* (Hay House 10th anniversary edition 2016) and Dr Joe Dispenza *Being Supernatural: How Common People Are Doing the Uncommon* (Hay House 2017).

saying. When we want them to not talk back, we have to look at how we have been speaking to them or how we speak to people in general that they have witnessed and become accustomed to. The more we understand what it's like to be in their world and are aware of what is going on for them, the easier it is to find ways of dealing with things and reaching them in more positive and beneficial ways for all concerned.

What teens would tell you if they knew

- **I need to know I am still loved, I don't care about what you know, unless I know that you care.** You won't have a good relationship with your teen unless they know they are loved, valued and you do care about them. Remember they are the same bundle of joy you loved and adored when they arrived. They grow and change over time and understanding that a lot of their behaviour is down to biology, the way their brain is changing and developing, helps us cope and deal with what's going on for them.
- **I still need hugs, human contact.** You may say your teen doesn't like hugs, doesn't want you to be openly affectionate and this may be true. Think why this might be the case. When did it change? Chances are you changed your attitude to them at some point. How confusing is it for children? Keep hugging, encourage it. Hugging stimulates the brain to release oxytocin, known as the "calming and closeness hormone"[4] (produced by the hypothalamus, delivered to the pituitary gland and then released into the body).

---

[4] Kerstin Uvnäs Moberg *The Hormone of Closeness: The Role of Oxytocin in Relationships* (Pinter & Martin 2013).

- **I need more sleep than you and am not tired when you are!** The growth hormone is released during sleep and they grow at such a rapid rate, they need a lot of sleep for the hormone to be released. Studies show the sleep hormone melatonin is released around 1.00a.m in teenagers and not around 10.00p.m. as in most adults so they are not tired or ready for bed when you are, or when you want them to be.
- **I need a calm environment (even if I don't think I do).** We've already established teenagers don't feel the need to go to bed, or sleep as early as we might want them to, so providing a calm environment for them before this time is important. They respond to outside stimulus and a noisy household, TV or music blaring out, arguments, tension or any unpleasant atmosphere has an effect on them. They pick up the energy of it and remain stimulated at a time when we want the least amount of stimuli to get them in the right place to start to begin to get ready for sleep.
- **I need you to talk with me, or to me and not at me.** Somehow we lose sight of our teenagers as other people. Ask yourself when you've said something to them or spoken to them in a certain way, "Would I speak to anyone else like that?" Speak to them as you want to be spoken to, with patience and respect. You may be thinking they don't speak to me like that. You set the example first. If you want to see the change, be the change. When we speak to our teenagers, they may be listening (or not!) though not hearing us. Because there is still confusion going on in the teenage brain, they can often misinterpret facial expressions and misread what you are saying to them. Make sure your mouth and face are saying the same thing! Ask if

they have heard you, ask if they have understood and to make sure they have, ask them to repeat it back to you. You'll be amazed at what they think you've said sometimes!

- **I'm not clumsy, I just don't know where the end of my limbs are!** As funny as that might sound, they don't. They are growing at such speed, their brain hasn't caught up or got used to their lengthened limbs yet and as they reach for things they can knock them over, or trip up stairs or down, not yet knowing where they end! Be patient and understanding, not critical. The last thing they need to hear is they're stupid or clumsy for behaviour they cannot help. I like this quote I once saw, something a teenager might say: "I'm not clumsy, it's just the floor hates me, the tables and chairs are bullies and the wall gets in the way!"

- **I need you to share new things with me.** Although you may say your teenagers aren't interested in sharing anything with you, as long as you continue to share experiences with your child from a young age they will continue to enjoy it and even if you haven't done so for a while, when you show your teenager you are willing and interested in learning new things and having new experiences, it will keep them interested, arouse their curiosity and appeal to their sense of wanting new experiences. Doing different things helps their brain grow. Suggest juggling, trampolining, D.I.Y., painting pictures or decorating. The more you do and expose them to the more that will be their norm and they are affected by what surrounds them, the environment and experiences they are exposed to.

- **It's important to me that you show interest in and respect what I like and am interested in.** It's easy to "dis" what our teenagers are interested in, such as awful music or dreadful fashion styles. It's important to remember that this is our opinion, it's their life, their body (difficult when they are having tattoos or piercings we don't approve of!). Be positive, find something good to say, it helps them and their brain to feel good. If they constantly hear disapproval, complaining, dissatisfaction from you, they run neural pathways that wire together to form a programme that they will come to know and when they feel you always react that certain (negative) way they stop communication and you lose connection, distance happens and the relationship breaks down.

- **I need to feel important and valued so ask my opinion and honour my choices.** When good habits are formed with your children early on it's easier to keep the momentum. When you allow your children to make choices when they are young, simple choices, and whichever they choose you are happy with, like what would you like for tea, pizza or chicken, they start to be confident in decision making. This can continue into teenage years. If you haven't done it so far, start. They need to learn to make choices and decisions. Let their brain have the opportunity to use its abilities, instead of making their mind up for them or being too dictatorial.

- **Don't tell me I can't or I'm not allowed to (it's not true!).** The teenage brain has a need for instant gratification and reward and isn't too good at seeing the danger in things or the consequences of certain actions. If your teen decides to do something you think is dangerous and would rather they didn't, be careful of your initial response. To yell "Oh no you're not" is likely to promote an "Oh yes I am" or "You can't stop me" response, not conducive to having a calm and sensible discussion about it. Remain calm, respond rather than react and ask helpful questions like "Have you considered what might happen if..." or "Have you looked into it properly, researched it?" Simply have a discussion about it. Understanding that the reason they want to seek out these thrills is because their brain is wired to at this age at least helps you understand them a bit better. Saying "You can't" isn't really true or what we mean, we usually mean "I would rather you didn't!" When teenagers say "I can't..." in relation to doing something in a defeatist way, it's good to encourage them by saying "You can't do that... yet" or "You haven't learn to yet, that's all."

- **I can feel the mood you're in whether you're saying so or not!** We all emit an energetic vibration. Research from the institute of Heartmath tells us our heart can radiate an electromagnetic field that can reach others and affects them.[5] Our thoughts are an energetic impulse and they too can be measured. So the vibration we give out is measurable and can be felt by others. Children are very good at picking up this energy, this truth of our feelings, our thoughts and our emotional state, whatever we are saying. So it's important that thoughts and feelings match what we are saying.

- **Be fair with me, treat me and speak to me as you would others.** This is something we tend to forget, how to treat our teenagers as people. Think for a minute how you speak to them, tell them to do things, threaten them, shout, etc., then imagine

---

[5] *Science of the Heart: Exploring the Role of the Heart in Human Performance* (The Institute of Heartmath 2016) at www.heartmath. org/?sid=3088&s=science+of+the+heart [accessed April 2020].

it was a friend of yours. Would you behave the same way, speak in the same manner? Probably not. We forget that our teenagers are growing into adults and deserve the same consideration as other adults. Because they are family, that's no excuse to behave in an unacceptable way. Be consistent in the way you ask anyone to do something for you, or tell them something.

- **Ask me "Why?" and I probably won't know.** Although asking "Why?" our teenagers have done something or behaved in a certain way seems natural, it's one of the worst things to ask them. It immediately causes a defensive answer; think about how you feel if someone asks you why you've done something, doesn't it feel a bit like criticism and put you on the defensive? It prompts a story or an excuse or a defensive answer. Much better to ask, in a calm and measured way, with genuine interest in the answer "What were you aiming to achieve when you…?" or "What outcome were you hoping for?" Framed this way, the critical faculty of the brain/mind is bypassed, it doesn't immediately feel defensive and throw out a story. The mind will think about what you've asked and genuinely look deeper for the answer.

- **I'm not stupid or ridiculous because of the choices I've made, I just haven't developed the risk taking and consequences skill yet.** Our teenagers often do things we would consider dangerous, stupid or ridiculous. Things that often prompt the question "What were you thinking?" Fact is, they weren't! At least not like you or I might. Their brain won't let them… yet! They haven't developed the cortex, the thinking bit of the brain, yet. As for risk taking, teenagers are just looking for excitement and the thrill of something that we would probably deem too dangerous. Their brain is under construction and chemicals fluctuate and often the dopamine level is high, which leads to wanting more of the feel-good factor activities. It's not stupid, it's natural.

- **Tell me what you want, not what you don't.** We often tell our teenagers what we don't want them to do: "Don't" followed by "get drunk, be late, forget your bus pass, book, keys, phone" etc., and what we are doing is drawing attention to what we don't want and even putting an idea into their head that hadn't occurred to them.

- **Simple instructions please.** If we over-complicate instructions, or give too many at once, it overloads the teenage brain and they can't make sense of or retain it all. Remember that the prefrontal cortex is still developing.

- **Help me be organized, rather than criticize me for not being.** When we realize the brain is still learning to use the prefrontal cortex, we can help. Create a planner, a way to organize tasks, appointments, etc. If we show them how and help implement a strategy, it becomes embedded, a habit, and will eventually be natural to them. Consistency and patience are needed.

- **To you, it's nothing, to me it's a drama, the end of the world!** The brain is using the amygdala (responsible for emotions) more than the prefrontal cortex (reasoning and logic) so can appear very emotional and stressed by events that we as adults see differently. It's important to be empathetic and understanding here. No good telling them it's nothing to worry about. To them it is.

- **Help me make my mind up and make my own choices.** A teenager can often have a great idea that strikes terror in us, like wanting to go skydiving for instance. Rather than immediately lay the law down and forbid it, or fly off the handle, remain calm and ask if they have thought it through. Talk with them about whatever it is. Put your point of view over calmly and then ask them to think about it and the consequences. Remember it is their life after all!

- **Channel my enthusiasm for new things.** It's easy to say what we don't want them to do, so look for and encourage things you would be happy for them to do that they might not have thought about. The brain is in need of lots of stimulation so help them instead of leaving it up to them to find it.
- **I don't listen if it's only coming from you.** Influenced more by outsiders than you, it helps get a message across or make a point when we use extended quotes, which means saying what you want to say as though someone else has said it or experienced it. For example, the woman in the supermarket was telling the checkout girl that her neighbour had said, her grandson had… then tell a story illustrating your point. It goes in at a deeper level, after all it's not you telling them.

Attachment theory

Some behaviours exhibited in children and young people can be traced back to them having attachment disorder. If their early experiences were not positive ones, or their early bonding and connecting with their primary caregiver was fragile, not established or even negative, they can form an attachment disorder.[6]

---

[6] Davenport Child Development and McCartney and Phillips Early Childhood Development.

The dictionary definition of attachment is "an extra part or extension that is or may be attached to something to perform a particular function".[7] This is how a baby feels when it's born, attached to and part of the mother and it takes a while to understand that it isn't.

A further definition is "affection, fondness, or sympathy for someone or something". This is the kind of attachment that we want to aim for. We want to always feel this with our children and them to feel it for us. I like the word connection too, we always want to feel connected to our children. As they grow up it can become harder, especially in the teenage years when they feel very disconnected from us and we from them. They often feel like strangers in our home, we don't really know them anymore, they behave and speak like aliens sometimes, from another planet. I know something parents often ask their teenagers "What planet are you on?" when they cannot understand something they've done or have said, or in response to some idea they've had that we see as totally ludicrous. They are on the same planet as we are, they're just looking through very different eyes. A lot is going on in the teenage brain that accounts for this. Other issues may be going on in a child's life that they are unhappy with and don't know how to handle, so it comes out in the unwanted behaviour we have to deal with. They could be being bullied, victimized, feeling peer pressure or media pressure and as this becomes too much for them and something they don't know how to handle, they lash out and behave in an unacceptable way. It's very important to talk with the child, have open and honest communication. When this has been put in place at any early age it is easier to continue with as children get older and reach their teens. It's still possible to reach

---

[7] www.lexico.com/definition/attachment [accessed April 2020].

a child or teenager as long as you have patience, are non-judgemental, loving and have ways of helping them to engage with you and communicate. Children have their own fears and anxieties, even phobias, that are very real to them. It's important we listen to them and encourage them to share.

Understanding attachment

How well your child does, whether they thrive or not, depends on their relationship with you. The bonding bit. This relationship has an impact on and affects them and their future. Their mental, physical and social behaviour and health. It is important to have a strong, positive emotional bond. Nonverbal communication is as important as verbal communication. If we are happy, positive parents this will be transmitted and if not and we are sad, depressed, negative, worried or angry, experiencing all these negative emotions, then this will come across and have an effect on our children.

I know my middle son has had attachment issues and struggled with feeling safe and secure and trusting, not feeling that the world is a safe place, and considering what happened to him as a baby this makes sense. Just weeks after he was born, his elder brother had a brain haemorrhage and was in hospital, and had to undergo several operations. His recuperation was a long process; after being on a life support machine and in intensive care for many weeks, he stayed in hospital for several more months and then had physio appointments, occupational therapy and speech therapy appointments as well as regular check-ups and further hospital visits over the next two years. I could not take Hal, as a baby, into the Intensive Care Unit, nor was it suitable to take him to the hospital once Kris, his brother, had moved to a ward, so he was left with a variety of different minders. There was no routine or consistency for Hal to get used to at this critical and very important time.

As Kris's recovery took a couple of years I know that Hal was neglected, not intentionally of course, though that didn't matter, the experience for Hal was the same whether it was intentional or not. He and I didn't get the chance to have the relationship at that time I would have wanted and expected to have. I was also, understandably, not in a very good place, worried and upset about my eldest son, and Hal didn't get the best of me even when I was with him. I was occupied with the huge event that had happened and what was going on.

Hal would have picked up on my state. I have repaired the situation, being aware of it and realizing it was the starting point. I have talked to him about it and explained all the above. I have used EAM for both me and Hal and put other good parenting stuff in place and we have a really good relationship, I am very happy to say.

I also know from providing supported lodging for teenagers and fostering that attachment was a big issue in their lives. Whether it's your own child, or a child you know, are fostering or adopting, be mindful that you may not know everything that has happened to them.

It is never too late to treat and repair attachment difficulties, though the earlier you spot the symptoms and take steps to repair them, the better. With early detection, you can avoid a more serious problem. Caught in infancy, attachment problems are often easy to correct with the right help and support.

Parenting a child with an attachment disorder can be exhausting, as can parenting any child, frustrating and emotionally trying and draining. Sometimes you may wonder if your efforts are worth it; be assured that they are. With time, patience and concerted effort, attachment disorders can be repaired. The key is to remain calm yet firm as you interact with your child. This will teach your child that they are safe and can trust you. Remember the following:

- **Have realistic expectations.** Helping your child with an attachment disorder may be a long road. Focus on making small steps forward and celebrate every sign of success.
- **Patience is essential.** The process may not be as rapid as you'd like, and you can expect bumps along the way. Remain patient and focus on small improvements, and create an atmosphere of safety for your child.
- **Have a sense of humour and have fun.** Humour and having fun go a long way towards repairing attachment problems and energizing you even in the midst of hard work. Find at least a couple of people, activities or DVDs that help you laugh and feel good.
- **Take care of yourself.** Reduce other demands on your time and make time for yourself. Say no to non-priorities, get enough rest, good nutrition, and parenting breaks to help you relax and recharge your batteries so you can give your attention to your child.
- **Find support and ask for help.** Rely on friends, family, community resources and respite care (if available). Ask for help before you really need it to avoid getting stressed to breaking point.

You may also want to consider joining a support group for parents.

- **Stay positive.** Be sensitive to the fact that children pick up on feelings. If they sense you're discouraged, it will be discouraging to them. If you're anxious they will sense it. When you are feeling down, or it's too much, turn to others for reassurance and assistance.

Tips for helping your child feel safe and secure

Safety is the core issue. They are distant and distrustful because they feel unsafe in the world. They keep their guard up to protect themselves yet this also prevents them from accepting love and support. So before anything else, it is essential to build up your child's sense of security. Do this by establishing clear expectations and rules of behaviour, and by responding consistently so your child knows what to expect when they act a certain way and even more importantly knows that no matter what happens, you can be counted on. That you will love and support them through their difficult times. Although we're addressing attachment disorder in particular, the following applies to all children.

- **Set limits and boundaries.** Consistent, loving boundaries make the world seem more predictable and less scary to children. It's important that they understand what behaviour is expected of them, what is and isn't acceptable and what the consequences will be if they disregard the rules. This also teaches them that they have control over what happens to them.
- **Take charge and remain calm.** Remember that bad behaviour means that your child doesn't know how to handle what they are feeling and need help.

Stay calm and you show your child that the feeling is manageable. If they are being purposefully defiant, follow through with the pre-established consequences in a calm, matter-of-fact manner. Never discipline a child when you're in an emotionally-charged state. If you react in a highly charged state and show you can't control your emotions then you're not setting a good example for them. You may also issue a punishment that you really don't want to carry out and may regret later and then retract. This sends out the wrong message and the child again doesn't know where they stand with you.

- **Be immediately available to reconnect following a conflict.** Conflict can be especially disturbing for children with insecure attachment or attachment disorders. After a conflict or tantrum where you've had to discipline your child, be ready to reconnect as soon as they are ready. This reinforces your consistency and love, and will help your child develop a trust that you'll be there through thick and thin. It establishes that you can separate the child from their behaviour.

- **Show you're human and initiate repair.** When you let frustration or anger get the best of you or you do something you realize is insensitive, quickly address this. Your willingness to take responsibility and make amends can strengthen the attachment bond. Children need to learn that you're not perfect either and despite whatever your behaviour was they are still loved.

- **Maintain predictable routines and schedules.** Children may feel threatened by transition periods and inconsistency, for example when travelling on holidays or visiting new places. As much as possible use a familiar routine or schedule to provide comfort during times of change.

Tips to help your child feel loved

A child who has not bonded early in life will have a hard time accepting love, especially physical expressions of love. You can help them learn to accept your love with time, consistency and repetition even when they reject them. Over time, they are likely to begin to accept them. Trust and security come from seeing loving actions, hearing reassuring words and feeling comforted over and over again.

- **Find things that feel good to your child.** If possible, show your child love through rocking, cuddling and holding, attachment experiences they missed out on earlier. Always be respectful of what feels comfortable and good to your child. In cases of previous abuse and trauma, you may have to go very slowly because your child may be very resistant to physical touch.
- **Respond to your child's emotional age.** They may often act like younger children, both socially and emotionally. You may need to treat them as though they were much younger, using more non-verbal methods of soothing and comforting.
- **Help your child identify emotions and express their needs.** They may not know what they are feeling or how to ask for what they need. Reinforce the idea that all feelings are okay and show them healthy ways to express their emotions.
- **Listen, talk and play with your child.** Carve out times when you're able to give your child your full, focused attention in ways that feel comfortable to them. It may seem hard to drop everything, eliminate distractions, and just be in the moment, but quality time together provides a great opportunity for your child to open up to you and feel your focused attention and care.

As I've said, all the above applies to all children. They need to know they are valued and cared for. Providing basic needs is obvious and remember to do all you can to support their health.

Tips for supporting your child's health

A child's eating, sleeping and exercise habits are always important. Healthy lifestyle habits can go a long way in reducing your child's stress levels and levelling out mood swings. When children with attachment disorders are relaxed, well-rested and feeling good, it will be much easier for them to handle life's challenges.

- **Water.** Plenty of water to keep them hydrated.
- **Diet.** Make sure your child eats a diet full of whole grains, fruits, vegetables and protein. Be sure to skip the sugar and add plenty of good fats, flax seed, avocados and olive oil for optimal brain health. It's worth looking at and possibly eliminating things that research is proving are not particularly good for any of us. Dairy products, caffeine, gluten. Buy organic whenever and wherever possible. Pesticides and herbicides are harmful.
- **Sleep.** If your child is tired during the day, it will be that much harder for them to focus on learning new things. Make their sleep schedule (bedtime and wake time) as consistent as possible.
- **Exercise.** Exercise or any type of physical activity can be a great antidote to stress, frustration and pent-up emotion, triggering endorphins to make your child feel good. Physical activity is especially important for the angry child. If your child isn't naturally active, try some different classes or sports to find something that is appealing.

Any one of these things, water, food, rest and exercise, can make the difference between a good and a bad day.

Having established the importance of the first few years of a child's life we can see how if this isn't the best start it can affect the behaviour of a child. There are many different reasons for them behaving in the way they do. Be aware of special needs.

Special needs – we all have them!

I think we all have special needs, we are all unique and wired differently. We will never find two people who think exactly the same or perceive the world in exactly the same way.

Be curious as to what might be going on for your child, the reason for certain behaviour. A lot of those reasons may be one of the problems starting with D.

- Dyspraxia: a child who may be seen as clumsy and be called so, not able to do the things that you might expect at a certain age, like using a knife and fork, scissors, holding a pencil or learning to ride a bike, may have dyspraxia. This can affect anything where their fine motor skills are needed. They may use their limbs in an uncontrolled way.
- Dyslexia: problems with spelling, i.e. reading and writing.
- Dyscalculia: difficulties with numbers, arithmetic, etc.
- Dysgraphia: problems with handwriting.

It's always good to be aware of these conditions and see whether you think your child is exhibiting any of them. This could be at the root of their frustration and behaviour.

We all have our own set of values and priorities. We all have our strengths and our weaknesses. Labelling people or children isn't always helpful, though often necessary within the educational and medical system in order to get the support and help needed. Eden's difficulties in coping with life and learning were upsetting for us as parents and staff at the nursery and the school he attended, they couldn't cope with his behaviour, so the journey of having him assessed and finding what was "wrong" began at an early age. I now know there is so much we can do to help our children that still isn't common knowledge or common practice. Little things can make big changes, like what I've shared with you in this book. Anat Baniel has a method for awakening the brain and transforming the life of children with special needs.[8] She writes of breakthrough results for children with autism, Asperger's, brain injury and damage, ADHD and other undiagnosed developmental delays.

A colourful way of looking at it

Doreen Virtue (American author, born 1958) talks about the Indigo, Rainbow and Crystal children, known as Star Children or Star seeds. They are children who have different (higher) vibrations in their aura than the majority of people. I know how tuned in Eden was when he arrived, still connected I believe to the invisible stream of higher consciousness that exists for us all to tap into, for longer than most of us are. Children until the age of around seven have a real sense of knowing who they are and live without the restraints that are soon imposed by society. Wayne Dyer's last book is Memories From Heaven about children who remember life previously, past lives and where they

[8] Anat Benial Kids Beyond Limits: The Anat Baniel Method for Awakening the Brain and Transforming the Life of Your Child with Special Needs (TarcherPerigee 2012).

have come from.[9] A lovely children's book exploring this is Neale Walsch's *The Little Soul and the Sun*.[10] British poet William Wordsworth (1770–1850) in his 'Ode: Intimations of Immortality' expressed the idea that we gradually lose our intimate knowledge of heaven as we grow up, saying that when we are born we forget our previous heavenly existence.[11]

Children are soon moulded to fit in and very often we are trying to fit square pegs into round holes, damaging them and denying them the right to be their unique selves. Children who are being born now, and I believe this will continue, are already of a higher vibration than previous generations and are here to help raise the vibration of this planet and that is crucial for its evolution.

I knew my beautiful little boy Eden was challenging all I believed was normal in developmental stages and struggled with lots. Language was a big one, not able to read or write three letter words when he started secondary school. I used NLP strategies and hypno-speak, and made sure to carefully construct what I said to him, and over time we achieved great results.

Hypno-speak for positive results

Hypnotherapy is not like you see stage hypnotists using, in case you have any concerns. It comes from Hypnos, the

---

[9] Wayne W. Dyer and Dee Garnes *Memories of Heaven: Children's Astounding Recollections of the Time Before They Came to Earth* (Hay House 2015).

[10] Neale Donald Walsch *The Little Soul and the Sun: A Children's Parable Adapted from Conversations with God* (Hampton Roads Publishing Co 1998).

[11] William Wordsworth *Favourite Poems* (Dover Publications 2012).

personification of sleep in Greek mythology, and therapy is self-explanatory. It allows you to be in a lovely relaxed state where you are able to let your unconscious mind listen. You have slowed your brainwaves and heart rate down and are in a lovely relaxed mood, both in body and mind. When we rush around in daily life, we are using our five senses: seeing, hearing, tasting, smelling, and touching and feeling. In hypnotherapy, you will be still, not doing anything, not eating or using your sense of taste, not particularly using your sense of smell and certainly, once you have closed your eyes, not using sight. You are still listening to the hypnotherapist's voice and the speed will slow down and the tone be very gentle and "You can start to really relax now...", an invitation to do just that. This is when the unconscious is more engaged and will take on board and reinforce all positive messages.

We squeeze the uniqueness and originality out of our children so we can squeeze them into boxes they don't fit in.

This technique and the use of what is called "Sleight of Mouth" helped me reach Eden. Magicians use sleight of hand and trick our eyes and in hypnotherapy and NLP the sleight of mouth helps trick the unconscious into hearing what we want it to hear: positive, reinforcing messages.

Language can often be ambiguous and cause mis-understanding, unintentional misunderstanding. In therapy we want to cause this, so there is a little confusion, and as the conscious mind tries to make sense of it, we bypass the critical faculty in the brain (mind) and get to the unconscious, where change can be made.

For example, I hope you hear here today what you need to hear here to hear just to start to begin now, to know now you can... confusing? Meant to be.

So many words we use, things we say, have more than one meaning. What about these?

He went for a tramp in the woods.

We are training specialists.

A revolver was found by the body.

Not clear, are they? Ambiguous and open to interpretation.

I started to incorporate hypnotherapy when I was putting Eden to bed at night and in the morning as he woke up, because the mind is very receptive at these times.

I used assumptions and mind reads, instead of questions.

Assumptions are used to pretend you already know something that is beneficial to know, before launching into what you are going to say, e.g. "I know, you'd rather be doing something else and I understand that, still, you have homework to do." Positive mind reads are also good, e.g. "I know you are going to have a good night's sleep and find that reading is so much easier tomorrow" or "I know you want to be helpful and put the pots in the dishwasher". We can use them at any time and as I said above, as your child is drifting off to sleep is a perfect time. As they are calm and safe and snuggly, talk to them in a soothing voice, gradually slowing down. Get comfy with them. I used to lie on the bed with Eden and establish rapport. Having good rapport means feeling the connection with someone, being in harmony with them, feeling an alikeness. Often when strangers meet it can be a little awkward, we don't know the other person, then we find out they went to the same school as us, lived somewhere we have lived, know someone we know. That brings us closer, we are more alike then. It breaks the ice and deeper connections can be made, it's more comfortable. We like to feel this sense of connection with others. People often congregate or group together because of the way they dress or an interest they have. It's a sense of belonging and it's reassuring. We can create rapport and there are many ways we can do this. We need to become more like the other person and match them in some way. This is helpful when we really want to connect with our child.

Ways to create rapport:

- We can match the other person's breathing. Watch when they breathe in and do it at the same time, breathe out when they do, get in the same breathing rhythm.
- Copy their movements (not so it's obvious!); make a smaller move than they have at the same time so you are matching them, or mirroring them. Matching means if they move and reposition their right arm, you do the same (a similar, smaller move) with your right arm. To mirror, imagine you are a mirror image of them, a reflection and you would then use your left arm to mirror their right arm move.
- Speak at a similar pace, tone, volume and intonation, matching their speech pattern. Again not too obviously, discreetly.

They will feel comfortable with you and find themselves liking you and not knowing why.

Building rapport with our children is important and can be done in subtle ways. As I said, I would lie next to Eden and mirror the position he was in as best I could, get into the same rhythm of breathing as him and speak at a similar pace and volume. Matching him, breathing at the same rate, speaking or moving as he did and then take the lead so he would follow me and then s-l-o-w everything down. As Eden was struggling at school, especially with reading and writing. I would reassuringly talk to him saying something like this:

"I know how it can be sometimes difficult for you at school and I know you are doing your best and you are getting better. Better and better every day, all the time… and I'm wondering just how good you'll feel when you realize that spelling is getting easier and easier every day for you and how you start to actually enjoy it. It becomes fun because you can do it better and better every day… and as you drift off now, you can imagine yourself doing really well with things that used to be hard (implying they no longer are) for you to do… you do it right now and well now…"

You'll notice that last sentence isn't complete, it's fractured with underlying implications. We are encouraging the conscious mind to look for meaning, make it make sense, and as this happens we bypass the critical faculty. The critical faculty is what divides the conscious and unconscious mind. As children we can switch easily between the two and go into the world of pretend and imagination. As we grow up, become adults, it gets more rigid and we don't bypass it as often. We want to bypass it to engage the unconscious mind, which is exactly where we want to embed these new ideas. As the mind hears these positive new suggestions (and you repeat them over and over, on many occasions) it will fire neurons and make new pathways wire and a new belief is installed.

Repetition is important. It takes time to find new routes in the brain. We need to practise this so we get comfortable with it and use it. I suggest whatever it is you want to help your child improve, you write a script and practise it. So they can easily use their imagination to see themselves doing whatever is suggested.

You may have heard the saying "practice makes perfect". I'd like to amend it slightly. Practice makes permanent. It needs to be perfect practice to make perfect. You can practise something that isn't good for you and then rather than it becoming perfect it becomes a bad habit. Bad eating, driving, drinking, smoking habits become so because we have done it over a period of time and it has become a programme we run. NLP and hypnotherapy can be used to uninstall programmes that no longer serve us and install new, more productive and beneficial ones.

I have experienced how incredible the brain is with my eldest son, who at the age of ten suffered a brain haemorrhage. I have talked a little about this previously. He was on a life support machine and in the Intensive Care Unit in hospital for months and when he finally came off the ventilator that was helping him breathe, he couldn't walk, talk or use his limbs. His brain's wiring had been well and truly messed up. It was a large bleed and injury and yet his brain found new pathways, new ways of firing and wiring and after a long time of recuperation, physiotherapy, speech therapy and occupational therapy, he made a remarkable recovery. He was left with some challenges and not the same as he was before and it took about two years of hard work. Because the brain has incredible plasticity, recovery is possible and as Kris was so young he made very good progress and recovery. The brain is an amazing organ. We do not use much of it and it is always possible to use it in other ways when we lose an old pathway or route.

I often use the analogy of the brain being like a large field of overgrown grass. We set out to battle through the long grass and it's very difficult the first time (like learning to walk); we stumble, struggle and get to the other side. We have made an indentation that first time and so the next time we follow the path it's slightly easier, the next time easier still, until after several journeys it's very easy for us. Now, if this pathway (habit) becomes undesirable for us and we want to change route, we have to create another pathway. We change direction and start the process all over again. The first time it's very difficult and the second time and so on, just like before, until we are flattening the grass to make an easy route and at the same time the old one (now less used) becomes overgrown and obliterated.

Inaccurate and inappropriate language

We've learnt how important and often inaccurate what we say is and remember when we say we know something we often don't, we are jumping to conclusions, assuming and using either cause and effect or complex equivalents.

Cause and effect

We've looked at cause and effect already. Where we step onto the *cause* side of the equation and not the *effect* side where we are a victim. We step into our personal power and know no one *makes* us do or feel anything. We can always choose (see Part 1 Chapter 2, Take control – of you!).

Complex equivalents

When we stretch our imagination and make something mean something that isn't obviously true, we are using a complex equivalent. We may have not received a phone call from someone with an address of a party we've been invited to and then make up stories of why not: "She hasn't rung me to give me the address, she obviously doesn't want me to go." It isn't obvious at all. She may have lost your number, her phone, been knocked down by a bus and be in hospital. Be wary of making stuff up, think outside the box what else might have happened. Do this with your children, think of other reasons they may or may not have done something and teach them to do the same.

Spatial language

As we've established, Eden struggled with language, especially understanding spatial location language, e.g. placement words such as behind, under, on top of or next to.

I often thought he wasn't listening to me when he was younger. I would give him instructions and he wouldn't carry them out, either at all, or not properly, e.g. "Eden please put your shoes on the top of the shoe rack, next to Hallam's under the coats." I thought that was a clear instruction. When I then found Eden's shoes on the bottom shelf of the rack, (not next to Hallam's, under the coats) I thought he just wasn't listening carefully, or had switched off and wasn't interested!

Or I would tell him what I'd done and then later when I referred to that again, he didn't seem to know what I was talking about, e.g. I'd tell him exactly where I'd put something, getting into the car I'd tell him "Eden, I've put your pump bag on the parcel shelf, behind you." Later when I asked him to get it, he didn't know where it was and seemed to not know what I was talking about. What I did learn after a lot of investigations into Eden's lack of understanding, remembering or him doing as he was asked (or told at school) was that he had a "pragmatic and semantic learning disorder or delay". That didn't mean very much to me at the time. In a nutshell, he didn't grasp vocabulary, including spatial location. Now things made sense. I needed to show Eden exactly what I was doing or what I meant, rather than just telling him and expecting him to know. There was more effort went into teaching Eden language than I had needed to use before with my older two and it was a good reminder that they are all different. What works for one of our children may very well not work for another. Eden did grasp the concept eventually and along with his diagnosis of Asperger's syndrome I learnt that he took things literally!

Eden had an odd turn of phrase and often didn't like the way other people worded things. When the doorbell rang and I would say "Someone's at the door" he would look at me quizzically and say "They're not 'at' it, they're 'behind' it", which, in fact, was more accurate.

On one occasion I came into the kitchen because the boys were arguing and Eden was really mad and frustrated with Hal. It was raining and all Hal had said was "It's raining cats and dogs." Well, you can imagine the argument that ensued then!

Daily life was a battle with Eden. He wasn't a happy child and it was a daily struggle to convince, cajole and get him into the taxi that would come to pick him up in the morning to take him to his special needs school. Even before getting divorced, I spent a lot of the time as a single parent, Adrian working away. I dreaded school mornings. They would go something like this. Manage to get Eden dressed, take him into bathroom to brush teeth, leave him to go and do something else, come back in and toothpaste all over sink, mirror or squeezed out somewhere! Attempt to clean that up as Eden would leave the bathroom taking clothes off, he didn't want to wear his uniform. Attempt to re-dress him, get him dressed, go to get lunch boxes put into bags, discover Eden making papier-mâché in the bidet, with the plug in and a full toilet roll turned to pulp! I'm not proud to say I very often lost it with him. I also know I ignored Hal at this time too. He was a good boy and didn't need the attention and supervising that Eden did.

I recorded some of the mornings and evenings I had with Eden so someone would listen to me when I was saying I couldn't cope. Heartbreaking to listen back to, bedtimes especially, when Eden is most distraught with his horrible days and hating himself. One of the mornings when I am so pre-occupied with Eden, Hal is reading his school reading book beautifully in the kitchen. I am listening though not giving him my full attention and say "Very good Hal", not really engaging with him or spending any time giving any specific praise, and immediately turn my attention back to what Eden is doing. It saddens me to hear this on the recording. Poor Hal, his needs weren't being met. Only weeks old when his elder brother had a brain haemorrhage, a period of being cared for by a string of other people as I couldn't take him into ICU where Kris was for months, then difficult taking him to hospital to visit even when Kris was on a ward. For two years Kris had intensive rehabilitation intervention and many hospital appointments and Hallam got neglected, though not intentionally, and I didn't see it at the time, though know now it had an impact and effect on him. By the time things had settled I was pregnant again and then along came Eden, who presented with what I then saw as problems, was very demanding and took a lot of my time and attention. Hal missing out again.

Sensory overload

Your child could be sensitive to sensory input. Children on the autistic spectrum (often referred to as Autistic Spectrum Disorder, or ASD) are. They are overwhelmed with too much stimulation of their senses, sight, hearing, smelling, or just too much activity going on. This causes them to behave in a different, what we might call odd or not normal, way. If your child often changes their behaviour from being in control to not being, look at what has changed, what's happened that could account for it. Monitor it and learn to understand what it is that sets your child off. There are children who are highly sensitive to other people's emotions, what goes on in the world, cruelty to animals, wanting to only eat plant-based food. These children and adults are often referred to as HSPs (Highly Sensitive People)

If a child is struggling to learn, the alphabet for example, or learning to read, write or count, it can lead to frustration and they will let you know. A child who acts the clown in class, or is cheeky, or causes trouble, is using mis-direction and distracting tactics to avoid the fact they are struggling in school or perhaps are simply bored, or can't engage. If they are bored, it could be that they have Attention Deficit Disorder. Investigate this, check it out and work with someone who is able to help.

Attention Deficit Disorder

I do think sometimes we use the term too readily. A lot of children who are labelled with ADD/ADHD (Attention Deficit Disorder/Attention Deficit Hyperactivity Disorder) often have one thing, a passion or obsession with something where they can sit and play for hours or spend hours engaged in and this means they have the "attention deficit" in an area that just hasn't grabbed their attention, isn't engaging their brain. Dr Edward (Ned) Hallowell has labelled this condition VAST (Variable Attention Stimulus Trait) and highlights the attributes of this rather than the disadvantages. There is an abundance of attention and it can often be all over the place, because of curiosity and an interest in so many things, rather than the one thing a child is being asked to concentrate and focus on.[12]

There are ways of helping children with subjects they are not too keen on, or struggle with, when we can use their preferred learning style (see Part 3 Chapter 4, Know your child's learning style). Eden was diagnosed with ADHD and yet he would spend hours drawing intricate pictures, making his own comic books or building with Lego or Knex. That held his attention. Many children are bored at school, the education system can't keep up, isn't made for them. It's outdated and not serving them well. I also know there are many fabulous teachers doing a great job and their best in limited conditions.

---

[12] Edward M. Hallowell and John J. Ratey *Delivered from Distraction: Getting the Most out of Life with Attention Deficit Disorder* (Ballantine Books 2006).

Ways to prevent
unwanted behaviour

Some behaviours are going to happen as a natural part of development, and then there are those that we have more control over and can do something about with the right attitude, awareness and strategies in place. The rate at which a child's brain develops is something we can't control, though we can influence it.

With a good relationship, mutual respect and an understanding of what the parenting journey is really about, how we can honour it, ourselves and our children and learn how to communicate in the most positive, effective way, we can avoid problems and situations that aren't because of inevitable brain development, learning challenges or conditions and can prevent unwanted and undesirable behaviour. Let's look at some ways of doing this.

Tell the truth

We often say things that aren't really true. Our unconscious mind is the part of our mind that knows the truth and takes things personally and it knows when we are lying. Just as a child knows that we often are when we say things like "You can't wear that today" (whatever it is) because, of course, they *can* wear it, it's just that we don't want them to.

If a child, teenager or anyone for that matter has done something, we may say "You *always* do that" or "He *always* does that" or "That *always* happens". Well, it's not true is it? It isn't *always*. It may be sometimes or even often; it won't be always. Always hasn't happened yet! It's a very long time, always. These all-encompassing statements or words like always, never and everyone are universal quantifiers and often heard from our children. "You never let me…" "Everyone else is going" "No one ever tells me anything". Be aware you may use them yourself. How honest are you being with your children or yourself?

We do tell them so many lies. Sometimes we mean to, other times we don't! Let's look at both the intentional and unintentional ones.

Intentional lies

We know the intentional lies we tell our children, the story of Father Christmas, the Easter Bunny, Tooth Fairy, all harmless you may think and it doesn't seem to affect them too badly, if at all. My two eldest boys coped alright when they found out this was fiction. Eden on the other hand went mad when he was told there was no Father Christmas. Not only upset at the discovery, mad at me for lying to him. He didn't understand why we made it up and he has a point, it's just as lovely to think that people at this time of the year buy presents for each other.

There are worse lies we tell children, like the bogey man will come and get you or some other scary threat if they don't do something. In a supermarket one day I witnessed a mum and little girl shopping, the little girl was curious as to what was behind the plastic slats that were the entrance to the store room, she was tentatively peering through and obviously inquisitive. Her mum told her to come away, she didn't, her mum's response, after a few times of saying come away, was "You don't want to go in there, that's where the monster lives." It had the desired effect. A few minutes spent with the child explaining what was in there and showing her, would have cured her curiosity. She'd have been educating her rather than frightening her.

We can often tell white lies, the ones that aren't really harmful or hurtful, e.g. someone rings you and your child answers the phone, you tell them to say you're not there if you don't want to speak to that person. It is still not being honest and you are setting an example to your kids!

Unintentional lies

We also lie to our children when we tell them they can't do something. Our children are able to go outside and play, paint or draw, use playdough, bake with you or some other activity. Then one day they ask if they can play outside, paint, play with playdough and the response is "You can't." That is confusing because they know they *can*, they have done. We really mean "I don't want you to" or "Not today because…" and then a reason, we're going out shortly, or we're doing something else. Be aware of leaving them with that phrase becoming wired in, "You can't." I overheard a neighbour talking to her granddaughter one day. The back door was open and the child was about to go outside "You can't go outside in bare feet" she said and the child did, "What did I just tell you?" my neighbour asked. What she had told her was she couldn't and that wasn't true and as the child heard it, it didn't process properly, she knew she could and proceeded to do so. Not as much in defiance as the unconscious mind knowing that wasn't true. The truth was my neighbour didn't want her to. If she had said "Put some shoes on before you go out", or given her a reason such as she might hurt her feet, the little girl might have.

When our children are at the stage where they're telling you they can't do something, suggest they say "not yet". Get your child to rephrase things for themself. If they say, for example, "I can't tie my shoelaces" "I can't do this" (whatever it is) or a teenager says "I can't drive", get them to add "I haven't learnt to yet", so it doesn't feel like it's them that's inadequate, it's a timing thing.

Calling it lying may seem a bit extreme, though that's what it is. When we say things like "You need to…" "You have to…" "You've got to…" to our children, most of the time they don't. In fact, they don't ever, as long as they are aware of the consequences and we are too. There is truth in saying "You need to breathe to live", though you can choose not to. There isn't that much else, really. There are the conditional "have to" and "got to" and "need to", the grades they have to achieve to get offered the place they want at university, or the practice they need to put in to excel at a favourite sport or discipline. This is all to fulfil a want or desire of theirs (maybe yours?). It's tough for us parents, often we want them to, we would like them to, though they do not *have* to. I'm not advocating soft parenting here, it's gentle, nurturing and truthful parenting. Because the unconscious mind knows the truth, knows it's being lied to at that level, the true essence of your child knows too. We programme it as we go through life to know we lie. How many times have you made a promise to yourself? New Year's resolutions are a good example. This year I am going to go to the gym, get fit, stop smoking, drinking, whatever, and then a few months or weeks in we haven't done what we were determined we would do. So over time our unconscious becomes programmed to know that we don't do as we say, it knows we lie to it!

Here's a scenario of what I mean about lying to our children. Your eleven-year-old son doesn't like getting up in the morning for school. You tell him "You need to get up now." Truth is, he doesn't really need to and he certainly doesn't want to. He doesn't get up, you shout up to him again from downstairs, "You've got to get up." Then you may find yourself saying "I've told you…" then repeat yourself or give a whole list of reasons why he has to get up now. We'll be late, you'll miss the bus, etc.

The truth is you want him to get up now so you can get out of the house on time. We've already talked about agreements, boundaries and consequences, so here you can remind him of agreements made around morning rituals and procedures. If they are not adhered to then we have the consequences. Consequences work better when they have a correlation to the offence; there has to be a relevance to teach something. So if your son won't get up and wants to stay in bed longer, he can go to bed earlier the night before to make sure he gets enough sleep. That makes more sense than taking his Xbox off him because he wouldn't get up. That's a punishment rather than a consequence and not really related to the incident.

When we say "I've told you…" there's an instant defence triggered, no one likes being told what to do, think about it, do you? Not really, it's no different to our children's unconscious mind. It doesn't need telling. You can say, "I have asked you…" or "I've already said…"; these are true and are gentler. Stay calm and present and aware and you will cope with any situation better.

We're all human and I know we use this language daily, need to, have to, got to, I do too. I want us to have the awareness and understanding that it isn't an absolute truth and when we have awareness we then have the choice to use different language that is more truthful and impactful and will help our children understand language better. How many times have you heard children say they need to? I need a new pair of trainers, the latest console game? They don't. I have to go to that party on Friday night, I have to have more money; they don't, they just want. If you use need to, have to, should, got to, etc. then they will too! You may also hear when they want something "everyone else has one" or when they want to go somewhere "everyone else is going"; however, of course it isn't really everyone.

How we lie to ourselves

It often happens first thing in the morning. What do you find yourself saying or thinking when you wake up, maybe "I have to get up, I've got to get up?" Even need to or should... not really true. I know this can be hard to get your head round at first and often in workshops I have someone who will not agree and say "Yes I do *have* to." Then we engage in a line of questioning that can go something like this:

"Do you really have to?"

"Yes, I have to go to work."

"Do you really have to go to work?"

"Of course I do."

"What would happen if you didn't?"

"I wouldn't get paid."

"And what's wrong with that?"

"I need the money."

"For what?"

"Paying my rent, bills and buying food."

"And what would happen if you didn't?"

"I might lose my home, my children would be hungry."

"And what's wrong with that?"

"I don't want to lose my home or my children to be hungry."
(Maybe getting a little exasperated with me by now!)

"So you go to work because you want to have a roof over
you and your children's heads and be able to buy food?"

"Yes."

"Then that's the reason you are getting up, it's the choice
you make to get up so you can go to work and will get paid
and can do what you want to do."

I want us to own what we do and that it is always a choice,
not a have to or got to from any external, outside force. We
have made the decision, we are using our personal power
and making choices, being at cause and owning it. It's not
someone else's fault. When we stop blaming and own it, it's
a much more empowering position.

Stop "should"ing

Being told or scolded with should can create barriers. It can
elicit resentment and defensiveness. Think about how you

feel when somebody tells you you should do something. How do they know? In fact how do you know something? We very often claim to know something when in fact we are really just choosing to believe it. I don't actually know whether the world is round or flat, I am choosing to believe that the images and photographs I've seen are true. I don't really know how old I am, I choose to believe the date on my birth certificate is correct. We often incorrectly identify what we call proof.

Find a different way of saying "You should be up now" when your teenager is still in bed at three in the afternoon, it could elicit a response like "what for?" or "why?" (assuming there isn't anywhere they are going or anything in particular they are doing). Be honest and say "I want you to get up now because..." then fill in the reason you do want them up. With a younger child, you may say something like "You shouldn't do that..." and often with no further explanation. If asked why or why not by a child then to say "Just because" or "Because I said so" isn't enough, their mind needs a better reason and that's how they'll learn, when the why not is explained to them. This creates a different relationship than the one you'll have when you are constantly telling them what they should do.

Be aware and beware of:

- should
- have to
- got to
- ought to
- must

Instead, use:

- could
- it might be better if you

- I'd probably do
- have you thought about
- I'd like you to

Here are four useful questions to ask yourself before opening your mouth:

1. How do I feel when told I "should" do something, or when someone says you "need" to do something? Put yourself in their shoes.
2. What was I like at this age, how might they be feeling?
3. What reason are they doing whatever it is they're doing?
4. When I say "You can't…" is it really true? They probably can do whatever it is they want to do, you just don't want them to.

Tattoos and ear tunnels

My middle son, Hal, has tattoos and ear tunnels. There are parents who would probably say these are things he shouldn't have done. The initial response to the tattoos was completely different from his father and I. We both saw them first on Facebook and we both posted comments. I was taken aback and wrote "Wow, did it hurt?", showing interest and not being judgmental. His father's comment was, "Dumb, don't tell me…"

Hal felt completely different about those responses. In fact his father didn't want to speak to Hal for a while (and vice versa!) and was furious he'd had tattoos. In his opinion he was ruining himself, and he believed Hal shouldn't have had them in case he comes to regret it later in life. That, of course, is not how Hal sees it. He can only live in the now and whatever he chooses to do now is right for him. Remembering the rose coloured specs here was good for me too. I remember thinking Hal's still got his arms, he hasn't had an accident and lost them. He's still here and for that I am grateful.

Some parents may well feel that they don't have to explain or justify the reason, though when you do explain or share your reasons with your child, it helps foster a relationship where they know you talk to them, spend time explaining and that you value them understanding the reasons for things. This keeps you closer and in later years, they will be more used to and willing to keep talking with you. Remember earlier I asked you to think about who changes in the child/adult relationship when they are continuing to do the things that were once acceptable, cute or funny. They behave a certain way for a certain amount of time and it is acceptable and then it isn't any more! They have to stop doing what they had been doing. We change the rules, we decide to do things differently. Consistency helps children know where they're at. It helps them feel comfortable, reassured, confident and happy.

Ways of encouraging wanted behaviour

Behaviour which is reinforced tends to be repeated (i.e. strengthened) and behaviour which is not reinforced tends to die out or be extinguished (i.e. weakened).

B. F. Skinner (American psychologist and behaviourist, 1904–1990) conducted an experiment with rats to observe operant conditioning. We have mentioned this before, where a certain event is in place and a response is made and then the connection between the two is learnt, i.e. baby cries, gets picked up and makes the connection between the two and then exhibits this behaviour to get the desired result.

Positive reinforcement

When we offer or present a child with something that they like, a reward, because they have done something we wanted, that is positive reinforcement. Skinner rewarded his rats with food pellets. He showed how positive reinforcement worked by placing a hungry rat in his Skinner box. The box contained a lever on the side and as the rat moved about the box it would accidentally knock the lever. Immediately it did so a food pellet would drop into a container next to the lever. The rats quickly learnt to go straight to the lever after a few times of being put in the box. The consequence of receiving food if they pressed the lever ensured that they would repeat the action again and again.[1]

Positive reinforcement strengthens a behaviour by providing a consequence an individual finds rewarding, e.g. if you give a child £5 (i.e. a reward) each time they complete their homework they are more likely to repeat this behaviour in the future, thus strengthening the behaviour of completing homework.

---

[1] Praveen Shrestha "Skinner's theory on Operant Conditioning" in *Psychestudy* (17 November 2017) at www.psychestudy.com/behavioral/learning-memory/operant-conditioning/skinner [accessed April 2020].

Negative reinforcement

Skinner showed how negative reinforcement worked by placing a rat in his Skinner box and then subjecting it to an unpleasant electric current which caused it some discomfort. As the rat moved about the box it would accidentally knock the lever. Immediately it did so the electric current would be switched off. The rats quickly learned to go straight to the lever after a few times of being put in the box. The consequence of escaping the electric current ensured that they would repeat the action again and again.

The removal of an unpleasant reinforcer can also strengthen behaviour. This is known as negative reinforcement because it is the removal of an adverse stimulus that is rewarding. Negative reinforcement strengthens behaviour because it stops or removes an unpleasant experience.

For example, if a child does not complete their homework, they give you £5. They will complete their homework to avoid paying £5, thus strengthening the behaviour of completing homework.

We can use either:

1. **Primary reinforcers:** these are stimuli which are naturally reinforcing because they directly satisfy need, e.g. giving a child an ice cream.
2. **Secondary reinforcers:** these are stimuli which are reinforcing through their association with a primary reinforcer, i.e. they do not directly satisfy a need, they are the means to do so. Pocket money does not directly satisfy a need but provides the means to buy the ice cream.

From conflict to cooperation

Most of us want to avoid conflict. It's uncomfortable, has a very negative feel to it and yet we seem to encounter a lot of conflict in our closest relationships. The incompatibility of ideas, desires and values is what causes the conflict. Often parents and children have conflicting interests because they have a different set of values and priorities. We can experience conflict at any age with anyone and in parenting it is often when our children are toddlers that we can have a battle of wills or, as is often said, when they are "flexing their muscles", and when we have teenagers. Also remember we can control outcomes by pre-setting the energy of a situation with our intentions and the choice of language we use.

How to avoid arguments

We often argue with our children because we're not getting our own way. Because they're not doing as they're told or they want to do something we don't want them to. I think it's often beneficial to think, "How would I deal with this situation if it was someone other than my child, would I say the same things, use the same language?" Probably not; we tend to think that because they are our children we have a right to speak to them as we like, say things to them we wouldn't dream of saying to another individual. So why do we think it's okay to speak to them this way? I know we want to keep them safe and have them respect us, or our rules if you like. Though, as rules are there to be tested, pushed, bent if not broken, it is better to have agreements already in place. Make agreements as to what is and isn't acceptable, what will and won't be tolerated, and have the consequences when expected behaviour is reached. In this way, children know they are heard, valued and they know they have agreed, rather than shouting back, when they've not stuck to them, "It's not fair" "You're so mean". You can remind them they agreed and are going back on their word. Keeping their word will be important to them as long as it's a value you have. If you go back on your word, they will see this, so it's important that you do as you say. This is important when it comes to boundaries. It's no good saying you will do something if you don't carry it out! I had a friend who, when his children were growing up, would say for example "You better have your coat on, or be ready by the time I count to three." He would often count to three and... nothing! That just taught he didn't do what he said he'd do.

Drop the interrogation

Rather than start a conversation by interrogating your children, say (declare) how you feel, what you're thinking.

Why w words won't work!

The w words I mean are why, when, who, what and where. These are interrogatives. We're interrogating our children when we start a question with any of these. For instance:

"Why on earth...?"

"When are you ever going to learn...?"

"Who do you think you are...?"

"What did you think you were doing...?"

"Where do you think you're going...?"

The reason it isn't helpful to start a conversation this way is because they feel threatened and automatically go into defence mode. It's the unconscious mind responding, a natural response. Of course we'll use these words, it's just not helpful to start with them, especially with the negative energy that accompanies it. It will encourage a knee jerk response, a story or a flippant reply. Give them time to respond better by keeping calm, breathing, collecting your thoughts and using something like "I'm wondering (then the what or who) …", "I'm curious (then the when or what) …" or "I'd like to know/hear/understand…". These are declaratives. You respond rather than react and give them time to formulate a response to your question or statement instead of a defensive or even sarcastic reply. You are starting with you and are declaring how you are feeling.

When we remember who we and our children are, human beings sharing a life and here to enjoy it, that we are in control of ourselves, no one else is, and that what comes out of our mouths is our choice, then it's easier to remember there really is no need to argue. Let's face it, it takes two. What good is there in arguing with your child? Debating something, where you are both putting forward your viewpoint, is a different thing. For every action there is an equal and opposite one, when you react to whatever has been done or said, then there will be an equal opposite one coming back at you! Avoid it. Let's learn to respond, not react.

Don't ask questions you don't want to hear the answer to

When being gentle, thoughtful and caring towards our children we often encouragingly ask "Shall we…" hoping to perhaps lead them away from an activity we want them to stop doing, e.g. "Shall we stop pulling the dog's ears?" or "Shall we leave the buttons on the washing machine alone?" Be prepared for a "no" answer. Rather than ask questions you don't want to know or might not like the answer to, offer an invitation, or more of a directive, say "Let's stop pulling the dogs ears" or "Let's leave the buttons on the washing machine alone", and depending on the age of the child, lead them away, re-direct their attention. Be ready with an alternative activity and use the word *and*: "Let's stop pulling the dog's ears *and* play with..." (whatever they like to play with) or read their favourite book or any other activity they enjoy. Also explain why we're not pulling the dog's ears anymore! When we make an invitation "Let's...", it's inclusive and a suggestion, you've put an idea into their head rather than asked the question and given them choice to say no.

Use tag questions

We have already discussed these in Magic Language and here we will look at them in more depth. These are questions tagged on at the end of a sentence accompanied with the appropriate body language, e.g. "Let's put all the toys away now, I know you can do a good job of that, can't you?" (nodding your head to add positive alignment). Remember that body language is a huge part of the meaning that's conveyed. "It would be better to do your homework now so you have time later to play video games, and you'll enjoy it more then knowing you've done your homework, won't you?" while nodding and perhaps even getting their homework out ready! Or "Let's put the pots in the dishwasher now, and tidy the kitchen, that'll feel better won't it?" Yes I know it can be considered manipulative, I'm not advocating that. NLP is sometimes considered manipulative, though it is a tool, like a knife that in the hands of a surgeon can save lives and in someone else's hands can take life. It's not the tool that's dangerous, it's how it's used.

Yelling and nagging cause deafness

Not because the decibels when shouting may damage their hearing, though they might! Because your children will switch off. They stop hearing you, or what you are saying, they just hear noise. The same with nagging. Neither will help you connect and communicate effectively.

When we shout, we've lost control, we're usually angry, annoyed, irritated or frustrated and that emotion is transmitted, the energy of it is out there along with unhelpful words.

Saying "Because I told you to" or "Because I said so" isn't fostering a good relationship, it teaches an unequal relationship, one where someone has more authority than the other. An interesting word often used is understand. Parents often ask, after saying something to their child, "Do you understand?" I know we use the word often, though the original meaning when asked by authority is asking do you agree to stand under me, be less than me, let me have authority over you? Interesting, isn't it?

Remember:

- To treat your child with the respect you would want to receive.
- That judgment and criticism aren't helpful or constructive.
- That to insist on your way or the highway teaches your child not to consider other people's perspective.

- Not to belittle, make fun of or dismiss their ideas or what they say.
- To look at what's happened in perspective, not blow it up out of proportion and make mountains out of molehills.
- Wear your rose coloured specs as often as possible and find some good in a situation. What might this lead to, what will they have learned? Remember life is about showing us all lessons to learn from, enabling us to grow.

Stop commanding – it's imperative

Commands don't work either; they're also known as imperatives. Remember to step into their shoes and how you'd feel if you were being commanded to do something. I often hear parents shout commands at their children: "Pick your clothes up", "Shut the door after you", "Get down here right now", "Put your toys away now" and using a lot of don'ts, too, e.g. "Don't you speak to me like that". Start with a declarative, that's starting with you, make a statement, e.g. "I'd like you to…" or "It's time to…"; you are declaring something.

Imperatives are not going to elicit a positive response or compliance as much as declaritives. They are dictatorial and don't show respect. Saying "Pick your bag up", "Close the door" or "Do your homework" is not as effective or polite as saying "I'd appreciate you picking your bag up", "Would you mind closing that door" or "I think it would be a good idea to do your homework now", and without sarcasm too!

Also using "thank you" at the end of a sencenetce rather than "please" has implicit effect. "I'd like you to do the washing up before you go out, thank you" has more of an expectation and assumption that it'll happen than pleading "I'd like you to do the washing up before you go out, please". There's a different energy in it. We sometimes forget that our children are people too and they deserve to be treated with respect.

Transition times – a bad time to question

Transitions times are not good times to be asking difficult questions or bringing up subjects that really need a quiet time and space and one where nothing else is about to happen. By transition times I mean when we're moving from one place to another, from one event to another with only a limited amount of time, like picking them up from school and rushing to get to a swimming lesson or football practice. Or leaving for school on a morning, already late and in a rush and restricted by time, possibly a little tense, stressed, wound up (you as well as the kids!). These are not the times to deal with other important issues or concerns and it is advisable to leave it. I know if I wanted to talk to my boys (again!) about leaving wet towels in a heap on the bathroom or bedroom floor, when they were leaving for school and half way out the door was not a good time to bring it up. Pick your moments with your children, there are some that are just not appropriate or productive. Arrange and organize the right time.

Another tip that can work is to casually ask a question you've been wanting to ask, or bring up a subject you feel would be good to discuss, when they are happily distracted. When they are absorbed in an activity, playing happily, perhaps painting or colouring in or when they are engaged in an activity with you, baking perhaps. Judge which activity is appropriate. As long as they seem calm and relaxed and feeling comfortable and safe, they will find it easier to communicate then. Judge wisely. Your child may well be absorbed and thoroughly engaged in some game on a console, or in an online interactive multiplayer game, and an interruption could cause mayhem. I know I have, in the past, attempted to talk to one of mine in this situation and if something doesn't go according to plan in the game and they "die" (apparently it happenes to characters in these type of games) then it will be your fault. "Look what you've done now!" or "I've died because of you"; not the best time to continue with what you were planning to ask or bring up!

Avoid punishment

Punishment isn't a word I like. Yes we need children and young people to know there are always consequences for their actions and they learn from them. There are different ways of dealing with children when they do not keep within boundaries and to agreements.

Although you may hear someone of the older generation say "I often got a clip round the ear or a good hiding and it never did me any harm", I would beg to differ. Even if you recover from the physical effect there will be a psychological effect and it will be different for different people. Still, it has an effect and the obvious one is that it teaches that it is alright to hit, to strike another person. It tends not to actually prevent the behaviour that it is being administered for. When a child is hit or spanked they may well know they don't like it or want it and can even become frightened of the adult who is responsible for it. It hasn't helped them look at the behaviour and work out another way of dealing with it. Have a discussion with them about what they have done and find out the reasons behind it.

What were they thinking would happen, what was it they were hoping to achieve?

Punishment is used as a deterrent though it often doesn't work. Our prisons are full of reoffenders and it doesn't always seem to put inmates off reoffending. It's better to make the consequences of our children's behaviour understood and then they pay a price, preferably a pre-agreed price, rather than be punished.

Problems with punishment

Research shows that children who are physically punished often go on to be more physical and violent than those who are not. Punished behaviour

- is not forgotten, it's suppressed; the behaviour returns when punishment is no longer present.
- causes increased aggression, it shows that aggression is a way to cope with problems.
- creates fear that can generalize to undesirable behaviours, e.g. fear of school, parents, authority.
- does not necessarily guide toward desired behaviour. Redirection and reinforcement tell you what to do, punishment only tells you what not to do.

The following is a story that illustrates how our children are so easily programmed and an example of punishment. Sitting in my first-floor apartment with the French windows open, I could see a car pull into the car park and hear what went on. The adults got out of the car with shopping to take to their apartment door, and their three-year-old was clambering out of the car from the back driver's side. She stopped to investigate the mechanism of the car door around the lock and was poking it, sticking something in it, and she was told to stop. She didn't stop, she carried on, she was then told "Do that one more time and you'll get a smacked leg." I watched her look at the adult. She paused for a moment and then returned to mess with the door again! She got the smack she was promised and then proceeded to cry, getting almost dragged into the flat with the adult saying "Just stop that, I told you to stop, you should have done what you were told."

Ok, a difficult situation. What would have been more productive was the adult explaining the reason it was a good idea to stop: it was dangerous, she could hurt herself, could stop the door working properly, and perhaps that would have made more sense than just "Stop." Then to admonish her for not doing as she is told is sending that message that we must do as we are told. Because we know the brain wires together the neurons that are fired together, if this is a repeated phrase in her life, she will grow up with that belief, that programming that "We must do as we are told." I don't think that is a particularly helpful thing for children to grow up believing. We must do as we are told, when? All the time? How about asking for something rather than telling? Asking her to stop and explaining why could have had a different outcome. If not, then absolutely explain what the consequences will be, not smacking though in my opinion. They could have helped the situation by explaining the reason why they were asking her to stop, directing her to another activity, engaging her, giving her an item of shopping to help with and involving her in what they were doing.

A while later the child was out, happily playing in sand in the car park and pouring it from one hand to the other, saying to herself over and over again "How dare you do, how dare you do...!" An adult came out and asked "What are you saying that for?" She didn't get a reply. She was saying it because that's a phrase she has heard, learnt and is now using, it's become part of her repertoire. She wasn't saying it to anyone in particular and wasn't understanding what she was saying.

Use consequences

Consequences are the results, the effects of something that has happened (or not). I think having consequences in place works really well with children, especially if they've agreed to them. When we've discussed the way we expect our children to behave, what's acceptable and what's not and also what will happen if that isn't adhered to, makes it fair. If they're involved in agreeing to the consequences, then if they have to be implemented, we can say "You agreed."

There may be occasions where you need to issue consequences in the moment, if a situation arises you haven't discussed. The important thing is to make sure if you issue consequences you carry them out, as I did in the following story:

Before I went out for my morning jog, I told my middle son, Hal, I wanted him to be up when I got back in, as I wanted his bedding in the wash. When I got back in, he wasn't up. I said I would give him five minutes. Five minutes later I went back in, he wasn't up. I then said I would give him a couple more minutes and if he wasn't up when I next came in I would pour a pint of water over him. He didn't get up and though I was dreading what would happen if I did it, I got a pint of water, went into his bedroom and threw it over him! It got him up, he was furious, went mad (actually put his fist through a wardrobe door, which he also mended later, the consequence of that action); he couldn't believe I'd actually done it *and* he now knew that I meant what I'd said.

He then got a glass of water and threw it back at me! I took a deep breath, thought for a moment and said "Just what I needed, nice and refreshing, I needed to cool down after my jog." I didn't react, I kept in control of my emotions, I talked about me and not him, and I also said "Did you know the walls around gardens in Spain are much lower than the walls around gardens in England?" You might wonder what that had to do with anything. The fact is, it didn't. It was totally irrelevant. It was side tracking and doing it changed the (emotional) state my teenager was in. It's a mind scramble. They get confused and you've broken the pattern. Confusion in the teenage brain is a common thing, it is undergoing many changes and understanding this can help us as parents understand a lot of their behaviour. My son often talks about the incident of the water throwing and says he really didn't think I would do it and then he couldn't believe when he threw some back at me that I actually thanked him and said what I said, the element of surprise! He definitely learnt the lesson too. Now, I know many parents would have behaved differently in this situation, though as I'm encouraging conscious parenting to build the best relationship with our child, it's important to keep sight of the end goal. If we'd have been outraged, furious in this situation, we may have acted in a different way, coming from ego and outrage. That wouldn't have been productive.

When boundaries and consequences of actions are firmly set down and the child knows this, then it makes more sense. Put them in place and do what you say you will do, so they know where they stand. They have security and routine. We've already said that a consequence is best when previously agreed, if possible. If it hasn't been, isn't something already discussed and put in place, it works best when it correlates to the "crime", i.e. there's a connection and a learning from it. If your child won't wear a safety helmet when riding a bike, then no bike is a fair enough consequence. If your daughter is speaking to you in a way you don't feel acceptable, grounding her doesn't correlate. If you decide you aren't going to speak to her when she wants you to, then there's a logical connection. Taking her phone off her for a set period, explaining if she speaks to you in that way, then until she speaks to you with respect you're removing the possibility of her speaking to anyone else like that. Reasons for the consequences help.

I know someone whose granddaughter wouldn't share with other children the sweets she had just been bought. The sweets were taken off her by an adult for being mean and not sharing. Although that seems logical, it doesn't teach her about sharing, it shows her that big people can have their way, can overpower little people. She was then going to my friend's house for tea, with the other children she wouldn't let have any of her sweets and where there was a tea party. That would have been an ideal opportunity for the adult to say all the food was theirs and they weren't sharing… when the brain/mind can make easy connections it learns faster. Look for opportunities to make the consequences as similar in meaning to what they have done.

Discipline

The word is from disciple, to follow, be careful of the reason we want our children to follow what we say or do. When we can explain or illustrate good reasons that's great, it's when we say "because I said so" that it isn't so great. Remember, our children do become our disciples and will do as we do, we are showing them constantly what we believe, what we think, what we value, as we live it. If we're not focused, if we're lazy, untidy, critical, complaining, angry and grumpy and then we're constantly telling them to be the opposite, it won't happen. Let's be the role model we want them to emulate.

Time in not time out

Very popular punishments for younger children are time out or the naughty step. Time out isn't necessarily going to help. To remove the child from the place where the behaviour has happened, ignoring the behaviour and telling them they will stay there (wherever time out is) for a set period of time doesn't help them address and reassess what they've done. Addressing and dealing with the behaviour, talking it through and delivering a consequence (preferably one that you have already let the child know will happen) is more beneficial. Calling somewhere the naughty step can reinforce a belief that they are naughty if they get sent there often, remember labels.

I think time in works best, stay where they are, talk about what's happened, spend time with them explaining what it is they've done that's not appropriate or acceptable and help them learn and understand this way. Reassure them that you can empathize with their feelings, that their feelings are not wrong, just that the behaviour is not desired. You can still put a consequence for their behaviour in place, if you feel that's appropriate.

Restriction causes resentment and rebellion

Be careful how you impose restrictions. Of course, impose those to keep your children safe. Though be wary of restricting their true essence, their spirit and their ability to be who they are meant to be. Allow their thoughts, ideas and opinions to be aired, consider them. When they are squashed, the spirit within the child will

You can't appreciate the beauty of a butterfly if you catch it and keep it in your hands. You have to release it, let it go to see its true beauty.

start to feel resentment even if they don't realize that; the unconscious part of them will and if it goes on, the resentment builds and can often erupt and be displayed in rebellion. Impose too many rules and restrictions and they will rebel. Discuss things with them, listen to their side and don't be too dictatorial. You will keep them close by letting go.

Teach your children to consider things, think them through. Let them know from an early age that you value their opinion. Avoid being prescriptive because you know best (or think you do), let them make their choices and learn to face the consequences. They will learn far more from their own experiences than they will from you telling them. When they know you value their opinion and allow them to contribute to decision making, they appreciate being appreciated and it helps foster a closer relationship between you. It helps them have a belief in themselves and confidence to voice their opinions and fly in life. One way of setting them free.

Respond rather than react

In any situation the way we behave has a knock-on effect as to how others will behave and certainly feel. When we lose it, explode, go mad or overreact then that is what we teach our children. We show them this is how you deal with unexpected and unwanted events. I know there are times when it's challenging to stay calm and I also know that when you are looking after you, present and mindful, you can stop, breathe, consider and really think before you speak and act. When you choose to be calm you are able to respond, not react. You are then response-able (it's where the word responsible comes from). Staying calm and really thinking about what you are going to say is important, sometimes we alert our child to problems they wouldn't even have thought about and we can be a bit alarmist.

I remember when Eden was due to move from his special needs unit of only nine pupils (separate from the main school), to go into a mainstream secondary school. He had decided he wanted to go there and set his heart on it, and he got there. The head mistress of the secondary school (of over a thousand pupils) was concerned Eden would get lost and not know where to go. She asked him how he would find his way around and get to class on time or find where he was supposed to go in such a large school with lots of different buildings. He said "Easy, give me a map." Simple! Out of the mouth of babes. We, as adults, sometimes put obstacles where there are none.

The benefits of responding

- It's far more responsible to respond rather than react, and responding is also more reasonable.
- For every action there is an equal and opposite reaction. So by reacting you're actually encouraging another reaction on the part of your child.
- Giving yourself time to respond allows you time to think and most of the time we make better decisions when we give ourselves time to think.
- Your child will be more likely to tell you things when they know you won't fly off the handle and overreact.

- When you make a habit of responding, they will tell you sooner rather than later about something they may rather not tell you about at all!

Six secrets to help you respond

1. Look after yourself first. When you make sure you are the best you first, you can then be the best in all the other roles you have in life.
2. Look after your health. Get enough sleep, eat well and take exercise. Not only will it help you feel better, it's great role modelling for your child.
3. Practise meditation, yoga, Qi Gong or Tai Chi. Take time to satisfy your mind, body and spirit. Pay at least as much attention to yourself as you do to your children.
4. Laugh more, enjoy yourself. Watch funny DVDs or comedy shows. Lighten up a little (or a lot!).
5. Change routines and habits. Be adventurous, explorative and spontaneous. The more you do, the more your child will feel encouraged to do the same.
6. Remember to ask: "For what reason did you do…" or "What was the intention behind you doing…?" before you start yelling: "Why?"!

When Eden brought a school friend over for tea and his friend knocked over a glass of orange juice, the child's face was one of horror and he froze on the spot. He held his breath and looked at me in terror! Eden quickly said "It's alright, my Mum doesn't shout when we have accidents" and I immediately backed him up. That child had probably been shouted at or admonished in the past and not had an encouraging or positive response to that kind of situation. What we do and say early in their life sticks. Make sure it's positive. What they hear us say about them to others and even the times we may have said something and think they're not listening, it all has impact.

One occasion where I behaved in an unhelpful way was when Hal was a toddler. He had had his afternoon nap and I thought I heard him awake, so went in to his bedroom to be greeted by what looked like a Christmas scene, snow everywhere! Well, thick white nappy cream. It was all over Hallam, his pyjamas, drawers, cot, carpet and he'd rather artistically covered half the window with it, making it look like a snow scene. I did not deal with it well. It was long before I knew anything I know now about responding well. I lost it, greeted Hallam with "OMG no! What on earth have you done...?" I was angry, I'm ashamed to admit. He didn't do anything wrong. He was exploring and experimenting and that is a good thing. He didn't know he wasn't supposed to do that with a tub of cream, there's no reason he should have. I had never taken the time to tell him not to do that, he had no idea it wasn't acceptable. I do know I shouted, not particularly at Hal, just at the situation and I remember Hal cried. I probably frightened him. Imagine the situation from his point of view. He's having a great time, busy having fun, being creative, exploring texture and feelings and smells and then I appear, not with a lovely smile and hello to join in with his fun just to react and show my displeasure.

Of course we want to put boundaries down and teach children what our expectations are and that there is a time and place for certain things, I just know I didn't handle this situation well and would have benefited from the "stop, breathe and think" method of responding and so would Hal.

Remember the 5 "E"s: Explore, Experiment, Experience, Express and Enjoy.

Sometimes, when we react, we are so focused on what we want to say and get out, or off our chest, we don't listen. One challenge parents have and often complain to me about is their children don't listen. I think they are listening (most of the time), they don't *hear* you. That can be selective hearing, i.e. they are choosing not to hear you because they don't want to. They've heard it so many times before, it's boring. They hear you and don't understand what you're saying and don't ask you to say it again or explain because they'd rather be getting on with something else. Or they mis-understand you, so they think they've heard you and know what you mean. Be fair and know that if they don't do as you've asked, it could be for many reasons. As Alfred Brendel pointed out, the words "listen" and "silent" contain the same letters.

> *Being able to respond and not react is like a willow tree that can bend and flex in the wind and remain rooted, when an old oak tree, rigid and inflexible, will break, snap and damage is done.*

Stay close by stepping back

Just as not being too restrictive and not having them tied to your apron strings will foster a closer relationship, so will avoiding telling them what to do or what you think. You can still find ways of getting through to them by putting distance between you and them. When we tell our children something, want to give them advice (heaven forbid!), they don't hear it or take it on board the same way they do when hearing it from someone else, we're too close.

So much of what we learn is learnt at an unconscious level and the unconscious mind is childlike, likes to have fun and loves stories. It also takes everything personally, so tell stories or anecdotes and your children will get the message. Extended quotes work well too. An extended quote is one that has a lot of distance between you and the person who originally said it. Rather than telling them what you think or what you've experienced, put distance between you and the information, e.g. "Someone I know, his grandfather worked with a man who said…"

The benefits of explaining your ideas through stories

- Stories, metaphors, anecdotes and extended quotes make more impact than telling your child something directly and saying it's what you think.
- We all enjoy stories. They engage the unconscious mind, they draw people in and they listen. In a story it's about someone else, not them (yeah, right!).
- Stories put distance between you, your child and what you're telling them, so there's less resistance.
- They will be more inclined to listen when you tell them it's something you've heard that's happened to someone else (even if it is really you).
- When they're listening to a story, it won't feel like you're judging or criticizing them, just you passing on something that may be helpful.

I hold a strong belief that what we're seeing outside ourselves is a reflection of our self, of what's on the inside. This may not be an easy concept to accept, and was certainly not easy to accept in the case of Hal when he was a teenager. He was feeling very down, fed up and angry, nothing was good in his life and everyone was against him, out to get him. He could see nothing very good about his world at the time. I told him the story of the village with the house full of 1,000 mirrors, visited by the happy dog and the angry dog. The angry dog goes into the houses and confronted with mirrors everywhere sees nothing but angry dogs barking back at him so he runs off and doesn't go back. The happy dog, on the other hand, sees only happy, tail-wagging dogs looking back at him.

Whilst my son may not have seen the relevance of the story at a conscious level and most probably went off thinking "What was all that about?", my mother's mad, lost the plot, etc., I am in no doubt his unconscious did get it.

Six steps to telling effective stories to aid your child's learning

1. Decide what point you want to teach your child, possibly the perils of smoking, and the consequences of long-term nicotine addiction.
2. Find metaphors for the features of a story, a white stick to represent a cigarette, barking for a smoker's cough, food that's gone off and smells really bad (something they really don't like) for smelly breath.
3. Weave the metaphors together to create the story and if it's abstract or ambiguous, so much the better for the unconscious to latch on to.
4. Add in another person (or two) between you and your teen to create an extended quote. "I heard this from Jean at work. Her father told her..."
5. Practise telling yourself the story a few times. Maybe add some repeated phrases such as "and the sound of that annoying, awful barking was even getting on his own nerves." Three is a magic number.
6. Accept that the story is unlikely to be perfect the first time. Remind yourself you'll get better at telling effective stories with more practice. Tell them with confidence, knowing the unconscious mind is listening.

My niece had cancer when she was younger and when she was going through treatment, I bought her a fluffy lamb whilst away on a holiday. When I gave

Using stories is like scoring a goal, you get the desired result after circumnavigating the pitch and a few detours, rather than scoring directly from one end to the other.

her the lamb, I told her the story of **where I'd** been staying on my holiday. I told her I had been on a farm, where from my bedroom window, I could see a field that was overrun with weeds. To begin with, I could only see two or three old, slow moving, scruffy sheep that weren't able to keep the grass short to allow the new green healthy grass to grow. Each day, new healthy beautiful white lambs would come into the field, jumping and bouncing around and eating the grass, keeping it short and healthy. On the first day there were only a few, then there were more the second day. As I watched them each day, new lambs would appear and do the work they were supposed to do, so the old sheep could leave. By the time I was ready to come home, the field was full of only lively, healthy white lambs and the grass was also short and healthy. Truly, nature at its best.

This was a great story for her unconscious mind to take personally. She has been clear of cancer for many years now, and if hearing the story and having the lamb helped her to focus on the positive and aid her recovery, then I'm happy. Even if you are sceptical about how effective telling her the story could have been, it has to be better to cheer up the child and get her to focus on something positive. And if the metaphor of the new healthy white cells spreading through her body played in her unconscious mind, when she remembered the story, it can only have been a good thing. The fact she had the toy sheep, a physical representation of the story, was a good anchor: each time she saw it, it triggered the connections.

Put yourself in your child's shoes

We often expect them to know what we know, or what we want! We expect them to be mind readers. Put yourself in their shoes. Really imagine standing in their shoes and go through a day imagining that you are them, see things from their viewpoint, how might you see things, understand things, interpret things? It's a good exercise to do. When something has happened, when they have done something and you cannot fathom the reason they have done it, before you go off the deep end, just wonder what they may have been feeling, what they may have interpreted the situation as meaning for them to behave the way they did. No one does anything without there being a very good reason for it, in their mind, and they only have, at that point, the resources and ability to do what they do. People are always doing the best they can in any situation. Do remember they have all their unconscious programming that influences what they do.

Conclusion

When I went along to my NLP course in April 2006 I knew I was not happy, was not enjoying my kids, our time together. I knew I wanted to change things and I learnt so much that I knew would help, though the task seemed overwhelming; there was so much to do, change and put in place I had to start with one thing at a time. Remember Lao Tzu, "a journey of a thousand miles starts with one step".

My first step was to list all the things I told my boys not to do, I wrote up three pages of things that started with "Don't". I had to think hard about what it was I wanted them to do and re-focus and re-phrase. Find your starting point and take it from there. I practised this for weeks before it became easier and second nature and then moved on to adding another element I'd learnt. Use your *Parenting Magic* journal for this: pick one thing to master, then move on.

Please be kind to yourself and your children. You don't get it wrong, you do the best you can with the resources available to you. Edison never got it wrong or made mistakes. On his way to making a light bulb that worked, he discovered hundreds of ways of not making that light bulb. Look what else he discovered and invented during that time, the motion picture camera, the phonograph, a battery for an electric car, and more.

You make the best choice in that moment and that's how it was meant to be. This universe knows what she's doing. If you are unhappy with something you've said or done, you will find ways of not doing it again. We spend a lot of time attempting to shape life and our children into what we think is best. Best for who? A lot of the time it's for us. It's important to remember they are not us. They have their own life to lead and whilst we want to guide, nurture and help them, whatever they choose to do is right for them at that time. We learn from all experiences, whether you consider them good or bad.

Remember

- People do the best they can with the resources available to them, that means everyone, including your children.
- There is no failure, only feedback; things that don't go according to plan provide valuable learning and indicators of how not to do it again!
- To accept the way other people see the world, even if you see it differently.
- Gratitude. You and they have achieved and succeeded in many areas of life. Appreciate that. You have so much to be grateful for.
- They have (as you do) free will and choice.
- It's their life. You are not responsible for how they choose to live it.
- They have their own personality and their own journey.

Remember Kahlil Gibran:

> You may give them your love but not your thoughts,
> For they have their own thoughts.
> You may house their bodies but not their souls,
> For their souls dwell in the house of tomorrow,
> Which you cannot visit, not even in your dreams.[1]

---

[1] Gibran *The Prophet*.

Six ways to be the best you

1. Have your own life, be the best you you can be. Look after yourself, do what you want to do, what satisfies you, with kindness and respect for others.
2. Live your life for you and include your children in your life, rather than living for them and through them. They won't always be with you.
3. Live a life, not just an existence. Experience it, cherish moments and celebrate them.
4. Be present and in the moment as often as you can.
5. Follow your heart and live the life you truly desire. It will fill you up and help you be the best parent you can be.
6. Love yourself and your life and you'll be able to love your children more.

Life is precious and passes quickly, enjoy it and your children.

The heart of the matter (the "matter" defined here as the subject or situation under consideration, i.e. parenting) is the heart of the matter ("matter" defined this time as a mass of physical substance, that's you!). When you are heart centred and heart feeling you will experience the connection that will send out positive vibrations. When you focus on your heart and take the time to connect with yourself in a calm and gentle way, you open the channels to connecting with your children in a more positive and productive way. You will benefit and so too will your child. Remember, "it is only with the heart that one can see rightly; what is essential is invisible to the eye".[2]

---

[2] Antoine De Saint-Exuprey, *The Little Prince* (Egmont 2020).

When you look after yourself first and do what's best for you, you will be a happier, healthier adult and oh so much more able to be the best parent you can be.

You now have plenty of new tools and techniques to use. You have your *Parenting Magic* journal to complete and material here to re-visit time and time again until it becomes second nature.

You have new awareness and plenty of ideas of how to Be, Do and Say things to achieve the results you want. To have a great relationship with your kids, to enjoy parenting and have a happy family life. To be able to pass this on to your children and to generations to come. To set them free and have every child able to shine their unique brilliance in the world.

Create your
Parenting Magic journal

Get yourself a lovely new notebook to use as your journal. Use this journal to record your experiences every day for the next 66 days... that's right, 66 days. Now you may have heard that it takes 21 days to form a new habit. That came from research carried out by Dr Maxwell Maltz (American cosmetic surgeon, 1899–1975), who observed a pattern in his clients. That it took at least 21 days for them to adjust to the change.[3] Now further research carried out by Phillippa Lally, a health psychology researcher at University College London, has observed that it takes 66 days on average to change a habit.[4] If you do something consistently it can take anywhere between two and eight months to implement the change and make it permanent. To be able to change your life that is very little investment and so worth it.

---

[3] Maxwell Maltz *Psycho Cybernetics* (Perigee Books 2015).
[4] Phillippa Lally, Cornelia H. M. van Jaarsveld, Henry W. W. Potts and Jane Wardle 'How are habits formed: Modelling habit formation in the real world' in *European Journal of Social Psychology*, 40 (6), 998–1009 (2010).

Use the template below:

Day and Date …………

My intention for today

……………………………………………………………………………………

My Action Step for today

……………………………………………………………………………………
……………………………………………………………………………………
……………………………………………………………………………………

What went well

……………………………………………………………………………………
……………………………………………………………………………………
……………………………………………………………………………………

Congratulations – now celebrate it

What didn't go so well?

……………………………………………………………………………………
……………………………………………………………………………………
……………………………………………………………………………………

What I intend to do about it

……………………………………………………………………………………
……………………………………………………………………………………
……………………………………………………………………………………

Congratulations – now celebrate that ☺

How to use your Parenting Magic journal

Enter the day and date at the top of your page.

Then write down your intention for that day, preferably a Be intention, such as be patient, kind, gentle with myself and others, non-judgmental, have fun, smile more, do someone a kind deed, pay someone a compliment, you choose.

Then choose one key point from the book, the one thing you are going to do today. We'll call this your Action Step. Something you will Be, Do or Say.

You will, as you become familiar with the tools, tips and techniques, get better and find yourself doing them automatically. At first, though, make the conscious effort to choose one.

Next write all the successes you had implementing that particular point or new habit. Celebrate and congratulate yourself.

On the second half of page write down what didn't work so well and how you could change that. Remember there is no failure, it's all feedback for learning and moving forward. Celebrate that.

An A–Z of Parenting Magic

Acceptance You have already accepted your children into your life, by having them. When you accepted that tiny bundle of joy into your life, you were also accepting all that they would bring with them, you just couldn't know then what that would be! I don't mean accept anything they do as alright, there have to be boundaries and consequences if they are broken. You can still accept them even when you do not accept their behaviour. It is really important to let them know that it is their behaviour that you do not like or approve of and not them, there is a big difference. When talking to a child, be aware of what you say to them and how you say it; what is said to a child has a massive impact and can stay with them the rest of their life. Keep their behaviour separate from who they are. When they have done something you think is silly, or even stupid, be clear and say "That was silly" not "You are silly". There's a big difference in telling a child, when talking about a specific incident "that was mean" and "you are mean". When a child hears something negative over and over again, insecurities and limiting beliefs are formed. Labels stick.

Believe in them. There can be a lot of negativity around our children. We are living in a world where there is a lot of bad news and they are exposed to it. Newspapers, news programmes, even listening to the majority of people's conservations, focusing on the negative, what's wrong in the world, and missing so much of what is actually good. If we as the adults get sucked into this we can influence them too, believing it's hard to make a living, hard to find a job, hard to be happy. We need to set a good example and let them see we believe it is possible to experience good things. So often children are put off doing things because adults tell them that won't work, or you can't do that, that'll be too difficult.

Confidence building is crucial. Encouraging self-confidence and self-belief will help them achieve what they want to. Not encouraging arrogance, just letting them know you believe in them and that they have all the resources inside that will help them do what they want to. I believe there is infinite potential inside everyone and it just needs releasing and realizing. As parents or teachers it is sometimes quicker and easier to do things for children when they are actually perfectly capable themselves. The sooner we let them have a go at something the sooner they will be able to accomplish and achieve it. Confidence means self-trust; think about a confidant, they are someone you can trust, so be your own best confidant! Trust yourself, when you do, that's having confidence. We need to encourage our children to have self-trust and grow in confidence. When they get something wrong that they're having a go at, find something they did well first and praise that. Then add the what could be done better bit! For example, the first time one of the teenagers I had living with me attempted making a smoothie it was messy. Too much fruit, hard fruit that wouldn't blend and no liquid. I wasn't present at the time, I came into the kitchen to find what she'd done. I had a choice in how I dealt with it. React, criticize and complain or respond and find what was good about it. I used the feedback sandwich, when you say something positive first (your first slice of bread), put in the filling, the how to improve it, make it better next time bit and then put the last slice on, finishing with an overall positive or compliment. So my saying "Oh good, glad to see you're having a go at making your own smoothie, that's a good choice for breakfast. It works much better with soft fruit and when you put some fruit juice or milk in too, so you can do that next time. Still tastes nice (it did), well done for having a go" is going to fill her with confidence and encourage her to try new things. If I'd gone mad at the mess, said she'd used the wrong fruits, used too much, not added liquid, got it wrong, that wouldn't have helped. Hearing this kind of thing often enough from the adults in their lives has an adverse effect on children, young people, anybody actually, and eats away at confidence and leads to low self-esteem.

Dreams Encourage them to have some. Not the kind that we have when we're asleep, the ones we have in waking hours, big dreams, hopes, aspirations, goals, whatever you want to call them. When we get clear about what we want, get focused, think about it, make plans for it, spend time imagining it, we are actually helping to bring it into existence. Quantum physics explains how everything is energy, everything, just vibrating at different speeds, and is made up of molecules, particles. Thought affects particles and draws them into your experience. What you spend your time thinking about will show up in your life, so think about what you do want, not what you don't want. The unconscious mind doesn't process negatives directly so even when you're thinking I don't want to be broke, I don't want a headache, I don't want to be late, you're bypassing the don't bit and focusing on being broke, having a headache, being late, all the things you don't want because you have to think of them to then not think of them! Flip it, think about being wealthy, healthy and on time. Help your children to identify what they really want to do and when you nurture a supportive, encouraging environment there's more chance they'll believe they can achieve whatever it is they want to. Just because a child isn't academically gifted doesn't mean they don't have other talents that are as valuable and needed. There are many styles of learning and we all have our preferences. They are not even consciously chosen, just the way we're wired. I learnt about learning styles when I did my NLP course and I realized that my youngest son, who was labelled with dyslexia and ADHD (also with Asperger's syndrome), was struggling with learning to read and write because he was a kinaesthetic learner (using the body). Often athletes, sports people and creative, artistic types who are good using their hands or bodies are kinaesthetic learners and struggle with learning the traditional talk and chalk way. Talk and chalk is still the predominant way of teaching. Teacher standing at the front of the class speaking and writing on a board or flipchart, meaning students need to learn through visual and auditory means. This is difficult for some people, they learn better through other methods, through doing or hands-on experiences.

Enthusiasm for what they are doing, even when you may not be so convinced it's a really good idea or may not work very well! If they've come up with an idea and are willing to share it, be positive about it first. Give them credit for at least thinking about it and coming up with something before adding any concerns you might have. When they have a great idea (even if it's only great to them) share in their enthusiasm. En-theos, relating to God and goodness.

Forgiveness There will be times they do something you would much rather they hadn't done. Depending on what that is, there will be different consequences. If it's a simple accident, forgive easily and quickly. My mother didn't find this easy. I remember breaking a glass bowl that had been my nana's, my mum's mum, and my mother went on and on about it. I felt bad enough for breaking it, it was an accident and yet my mother's reaction and going on about it made me feel worse. I remember my youngest son, Eden, bringing a boy home for tea once who knocked his glass of orange juice over, he flinched and looked at me quite terrified and waited with bated breath to see what would happen. Eden reassured him, "my mum doesn't shout when it's an accident". It made me wonder what kind of response that child got at home or elsewhere.

Even when they have done something intentionally that you do not approve of, decide on what actions you are going to take, what the consequences will be, calmly (or as calmly as possible) tell them and carry it out. Then leave it and carry on as normal. Make sure they know that you still love them, just not their behaviour on this occasion.

Giving The most important thing to give is love and time, not always easy, I know. We live in a busy, often hectic world where finding quality time to spend together is difficult. Family time is important, family meals are a great way of spending time together and talking. It's often where I hear things I wouldn't do otherwise, not only the things my boys are telling me, also the conversations they are having with each other teach and enlighten me. I get an insight into things I didn't know they liked, or were interested in, knew or thought. I hear their opinions on all sorts. It's very educational! Even when your teenagers are in the house and don't necessarily want to be in the same room as you, they still benefit from having you around somewhere. I learnt this from my boys, even though they would often be upstairs in their bedrooms watching TV or playing a game and not interacting with me, they told me it felt different when I was out, and even if we weren't doing anything together, just knowing I was in had a different feel to it. They liked just knowing I was there. Make it a habit also to encourage them to watch a TV programme or a film with you, and I used to make the effort to watch something they liked with them, not for the programme, just to spend time with them. In silence as I sit with them I send love from my heart out to them consciously and know it makes a difference. I practise Ho'oponopono (Hawaiian practice of releasing negativity): I love you, thank you, I'm sorry please forgive me. Parents often feel they have to give their children things, possessions, and do so sometimes as a way of relieving their own guilt for not being able to spend as much time as they think they should with their children because of work pressures, or just life's heavy demands on their time. Parents can often feel pressurized by their children and society into providing the latest gadgets, phones, etc.; this doesn't build the same bonds and relationship as giving of yourself does.

Happiness and the importance of hugs We want our children to be happy, we all want to be happy. Parents often buy their children's happiness, or the things they think will make their children happy. Happiness can't really be bought. Money can't buy you love, as the Beatles said, though it can go towards buying things that can help. Happiness is a feeling and if we continue to be only happy when we've got the latest new gadget or shiny thing it won't last. We only want a thing to give us a feeling. Happiness is truly within. Think of how happy a baby is with the simplest of things. Toddlers are often content and happy enjoying a cardboard box, rather than what it contained. They can get hours of entertainment and enjoyment playing make believe with home-made rockets made from boxes, or with furniture and sheets making tents, igloos, dens and hideaways. Their happiness is internal. They really benefit and grow when we can give them our time and be with them, fully present. The best present you can give them is BE it. Remember the energy that you are emitting is palpable and your child will feel that. They need hugs, positive physical contact. They are sensitive to your vibration and can read your energy. Be a happy vibration to influence them.

Inspire Be a source of inspiration. Be a great role model. Your children learn from you. The word means to be in spirit. Do whatever you're doing in good spirit. Lead the way for them in how to behave. Show them the way you deal with people, politely, considerately and always in the best way you can. In your actions and your words. Remember all the tips in this book for the best way to communicate and get the best outcomes in situations; when you adopt this way of being you are naturally inspiring your children to do the same. Inspire them to follow their hearts, their dreams, to believe anything is possible and to make the most of their life.

Joy and just join in They're not children for long, time passes so quickly, join in with their fun. You *have* got time to play with them, read to them, maybe not always, still you can find the time when you know how important it is. We all have 24 hours in a day, it's up to us how we use them. Join in when they are making a mess, whether it's painting, baking, making mud pies, be in the moment with them. My mum missed out (as we children did) on not wanting us to bake or paint because of the mess. Getting paint on a table or the walls isn't really such a big deal, it can be fixed. The missed opportunity for fun, exploration, joy and togetherness can't be. Remember to say yes more often, rather than no. Think of how to rearrange your sentences so they don't hear no as often, e.g. if they ask to go to the park, rather than saying no first and then offering the reason, be enthusiastic first and say something like "Oh what a lovely idea, I'd love to and we can go tomorrow or perhaps later today." It's not yes and it's not no either. Children often hear the word no so frequently it has a negative impact on their self-belief and self-worth.

Keep it simple When explaining things, only impart as much information as necessary. Say what you want to, make a point and then leave it. Keep it simple, no overlong or drawn out explanations are needed. No nagging or going on and on.

Listen Take time to listen to them and what's more, hear them. Give them your attention when they are talking to you, if you can. Know the time when you are able and prepared to listen, if not then tell them that, we always want to have boundaries in place and show them that we stick to them. Though if we are almost always engrossed in looking at our phone, scrolling, or on a laptop transfixed to the screen when our children want to speak to us, they soon learn (in their mind) they are not as important. I've seen it so often, a parent who answers, well barely answers, a child without taking their eyes of the screen and might say something like "Hmmm...", not an encouraging or engaged way of replying, is it? If possible, stop, look at them, acknowledge them and listen. Reflective listening is important too, say back to them what you think they're saying, or what you think you've understood. Get them to do this when you've spoken to them too.

Move Movement is so important. Exercise, it doesn't have to be a structured class, just something that is exercise for the body. Get outside, walk, take your children to the park, walk in the woods. It doesn't matter what the weather, dress appropriately and enjoy. There's no bad weather, just inappropriate clothing! They won't be motivated to move or exercise if you don't make it part of their lives.

Nurture them. Support and encourage them to develop in all areas of their life. Nurture a healthy mindset and way of dealing with emotions. Appreciate what they can do that you can't and ask for their help and appreciate it, this helps to nurture self-esteem, self-worth and confidence. It teaches them how to appreciate that too.

Openness Be honest with them about as much as you can. Share your feelings, what you are going through. We underestimate what they can deal with. If they have done something we're not happy with, explain that to them. Talk to them about how you are feeling because of that. If something is happening in the family, a close member has a serious illness, if age appropriate, find a way of sharing this, rather than keeping it a secret. They'll pick up on something being wrong and if we deny it and say it's nothing, they'll know that's not true.

Patience It's important to give our children time to do things rather than get anxious they're not potty trained yet, or reading yet, etc. When we are anxious or worried we pass on that negative energy. When you are looking after yourself, you can be calm and respond to things rather than react. You can keep your emotions in check and exhibit patience better.

Quiet time This is important for both you and your children. Incorporate meditation or quiet time for you into your day. Create some quiet time for the family too, especially in the evening. Wind down before bedtime, rather than expecting them to go straight to bed after jumping off a game or viewing a screen, they need time to start to get their brain waves to slow down. In the morning, too, have some peaceful time instead of straight up, TV on, or phones or games. Have gentle music on if anything, create a place of calm. Smells are important too, candles or a diffuser of essential oils help create calm, breathing them in lowers the heart rate and brain waves.

Respond not react We want our children to talk to us, tell us what's going on for them, share what's happening in their world and they are more likely to do this when you are a response-able adult, rather than a reactionary one.

If you fly off the handle when they tell you what they've done, e.g. lost their school bag, phone, wallet or whatever it is, they will avoid telling you things in the future.

Success Acknowledge all successes and encourage them to recognize them. Find them in the small things. It can be getting through another school day, if that's something they struggle with. Acknowledge achievements, there are so many every day. It might be they achieved getting up, getting to school, or for younger children, getting dressed by themselves, brushing their teeth themselves. Tell them, help them feel successful.

Thanks Give thanks for all you have, for them and all they do. Tell them what you are thankful for and say "thank you" to them for what you appreciate in them. Thank them for being generous, thoughtful, kind, gentle, for making you laugh, doing something for you. There are lots of things they do you can find to thank them for. Also use "thank you" rather than "please" when you want them to do something, e.g. "I'd like your coat and shoes moved now, thank you"; there's more of the assumption it'll get done.

Ultimatum avoidance! Be careful with them, in fact avoid them. They can be perceived as demands or threats. It's important we have boundaries in place and stick to them. When we don't, we are sending the message we don't do as we say and this can lead to them not being able to trust us. Even if they don't consciously think this, this is what the unconscious mind takes on board. Discuss the consequences of agreements or boundaries not being kept, so they know what will happen if they are not adhered to. Ultimatums don't offer choice, it's a case of my way or the highway and that's not useful.

Vocalize what you want and are thinking. Your children are not mind readers and often we tell them what we don't want them to do and not want we want them to do. Tell them what you want, you've more chance of them doing it. Tell them what you are thinking, share as things are happening and occurring to you, don't bottle it all up and then blow.

Welcome their ideas, consider them, encourage them. Give them time to tell you what they are, let them explain fully, without shutting them down before they've finished or dismissing them offhand. Then discuss the pros and cons. Have a discussion, consider from all angles.

X is for kisses Be expressive and demonstrative in showing how much you love them. We can be physical with hugs and kisses easily when they are little. Be aware there will be a time they go off this idea, respect that and still tell them and show them. Notes around the house, in unexpected places, coat pockets, lunch boxes, inside their rugby socks!

You Make time for you, do something to nurture yourself, refill your bucket, recharge your batteries. Satisfy your soul. Be the best you, then you will be the best parent you can be.

Zzzzzz Sleep well knowing you've put all this into practice.

Happy parenting ☺

Bibliography and further reading

Baniel, Anat, *Kids Beyond Limits: The Anat Baniel Method for Awakening the Brain and Transforming the Life of Your Child with Special Needs* (TarcherPerigee 2012).

Beckwith, Michael Bernard, *The Answer is You: Waking Up to Your Full Potential* (Sounds True 2009).

Bodenhamer, Bob G. and L. Michael Hall, *The User's Manual for the Brain Vol 1: The Complete Manual for Neuro-Linguistic Programming Practitioner Certification* (Crown House Publishing revised edition 2000).

Byrne, Rhonda, *The Secret* (Simon & Schuster UK 2006).

Byrne, Skye, *The Power of Henry's Imagination* (Simon & Schuster Children's UK 2015).

Davenport, G. C., *An Introduction to Child Development* (Collins Educational second edition 1997).

Dispenza, Dr Joe, *Being Supernatural: How Common People Are Doing the Uncommon* (Hay House 2017).

Dyer, Wayne W. and Dee Garnes, *Memories of Heaven: Children's Astounding Recollections of the Time Before They Came to Earth* (Hay House 2015).

Emoto, Masaru, *The Hidden Messages in Water* (Pocket Books 2005).

Ginott, Dr Haim G., *Between Parent & Teenager* (Avon Books 1969).

Hawkins, David R., *Power vs. Force: The Hidden Determinants of Human Behaviour* (Hay House 2002).

Hicks, Esther and Jerry Hicks, *Ask and it is Given: Learning to Manifest Your Desires* (Hay House second edition 2004).

Hillman, James, *The Soul's Code: In Search of Character and Calling* (Bantam 1997).

Lally, Phillippa, Cornelia H. M. van Jaarsveld, Henry W. W. Potts and Jane Wardle, 'How are habits formed: Modelling habit formation in the real world' in *European Journal of Social Psychology*, 40 (6), 998–1009 (2010).

Lipton, Bruce H., *The Biology of Belief* (Hay House 2016).

Maltz, Maxwell, *Psycho Cybernetics* (Perigee Books 2015).

McCloud, Carol, *Have You Filled a Bucket Today?* (Bucket Fillers 2015).

McCraty, Rollin, *The Energetic Heart: Bioelectromagnetic Interactions Within and Between People* (E-booklet published by HeartMath Institute 2002).

McLeod, Saul, Maslow's Hierarchy of Needs, available from www.simplypsychology.org/maslow.html [accessed April 2020].

Mehrabian, Albert, *Silent Messages: Communication of Emotions and Attitudes* (Wadsworth Publishing Company 1972).

NSPCC, www.nspcc.org.uk/keeping-children-safe/our-services/childline/ [accessed April 2020].

Rogers, Carl, *Client Centred Therapy* (Constable & Robinson 2003).

Rydall, Derek, *Emergence: Seven Steps for Radical Life Change* (Beyond Words Publishing 2015).

Schwartz, Robert, *Courageous Souls: Do We Plan Our Life Challenges Before Birth?* (Whispering Winds Press 2006).

Stillman, William, *Autism and the God Connection: Redefining the Autistic Experience Through Extraordinary Accounts of Spiritual Giftedness* (Sourcebooks 2006).

Stillman, William, *The Soul of Autism: Looking Beyond Labels to Unveil Spiritual Secrets of the Heart Savants* (New Page Books 2008).

Sutphen, Dick and Tara Sutphen, *Soul Agreements: Explain Your Life and Loves* (Hampton Roads Publishing Co. 2005).

Taylor, Yvette, *The Ultimate Self-Help Book: How to be Happy, Confident and Stress Free* (Infin8 Freedom Publishing 2018).

Tolle, Eckhart, *The Power of Now: A Guide to Spiritual Enlightenment* (Yellow Kite 2020).

Walsch, Neale Donald, *The Little Soul and the Sun: A Children's Parable Adapted from Conversations with God* (Hampton Roads Publishing Co. 1998).